23-50

ISOBEL BARNETT

PORTRAIT OF A LADY

ISOBEL BARNETT

PORTRAIT OF A LADY

JOCK GALLAGHER

METHUEN

First published 1982 by
Methuen London Ltd
11 New Fetter Lane, London EC4P 4EE

Copyright © Jock Gallagher 1982

Photoset, printed and bound in Great Britain by
Redwood Burn Limited,
Trowbridge, Wiltshire

British Library Cataloguing in Publication Data

Gallagher, Jock
Isobel Barnett.
1. Barnett, Isobel   2. Broadcasters –
Great Britain – Biography
I. Title
791.44'028'0924   PN1990.72.B/

ISBN 0–413–51320–3

AUTHOR'S NOTE

Now I know how a portrait painter must feel when confronted by a restless model. Lady Barnett did not sit still for this study. She lived her life in breakneck style and sometimes I have only been able to capture the blur of her personality as she swept along on a tide of enthusiasm. It is no comfort to say that few of even her closest friends had any more success in saying with confidence: this is the real Isobel Barnett. What, then, is on offer here is an impressionist portrait – the lady seen through the eyes of her friends and associates, through the writings of many journalists and not a little of her own. I am grateful to them all for their contributions and I would especially like to thank Rosemary Anderson, Jeanne Burton, Norah Cheatle, Daphne Creer, Elizabeth Fraser, Audrey Green, Sybil Lines, Andrew Marshall, Jack Meadows, Robert Shanks, Tony Shryane, Angela Stoneman and the Very Reverend Alan Warren. I would also like to acknowledge Hutchinson Books Ltd for quotations from *My Lifeline* by Isobel Barnett, and Pelham Books Ltd for quotations from *Lady Barnett's Cookbook*.

To Molly Cox, who gave so much help and advice, I can only say that Lady Barnett was lucky to have such a friend and I was very fortunate in having her co-operation.

The care of Pamela Relton's research and the tirelessness of Sue Marshall's secretarial labours was matched only by the patience of my wife. I thank them all.

J.G.

CHAPTER 1

*A*t the height of her fame and of a popularity unequalled by any previous television performer, Isobel Barnett was featured in a national newspaper as one of Britain's indestructible personalities. This was in 1961, when her success in the astonishingly popular 'What's My Line?' television programme, gave her – according to *Daily Mail* readers – equal status with three other women of significant achievement: Barbara Castle, the fiery, red-haired Labour MP who became Minister of Transport; Pat Smythe, the champion horsewoman whose partnership with Showjumper thrilled the nation; and Anne Shelton, the singer who topped the charts with hits like 'The Old Rugged Cross' and 'Lay Down Your Arms'. The four had been voted the country's most successful women of the year, and each was seen to have 'determination if not stubborness; resilience if not ruthlessness', qualities that would, said the *Daily Mail*, keep them at the top just as long as that was where they wanted to be.

To the beautiful Lady Barnett's many friends and millions of admirers, it seemed a completely appropriate accolade. Born of comfortable, upper-middle-class parents, a successful doctor herself, and wife of a wealthy businessman, she had taken stylishly to her role as a television panellist. Her charismatic charm and patent intelligence proved to be an unbeatable combination. As an addition to her long list of the glittering prizes, she had become one of the medium's first superstars. If her upper-crust elegance and almost glacial composure seemed to keep viewers at arm's-length, they simply loved her the more. She won the kind of affection and adulation more recently reserved for the Princess of Wales.

Those were the days when the masses liked to look up to their stars, when idols were still secure on their pedestals. Then, indeed, the glamorous Lady Barnett looked every inch an indestructible, with the world at her feet. A contemporaneous examination would have detected few cracks in her personality, perhaps only a somewhat exaggerated sense of propriety and an attendant determination to keep up appearances. She was brought up in a strict Scottish Presbyterian household and educated at a Quaker school, and her instinctive insistence on correctness made her seem very straight-laced in the *lassiz-faire* world of showbusiness. But that was countered by an infectious gaiety, a sense of fun and a readiness to laugh – especially at herself. Her anxiety about what other people might think about her seemed a simple idiosyncrasy.

Certainly no one could have foreseen a future for such a dazzling lady that would lead her to the shame of the dock in the Crown Court and to a desperately tragic death only four days after being found guilty of shoplifting. But if at the time her tiny flaws were seen as rather endearing eccentricities, in retrospect they were the cracks in her personality that proved to be so disastrous once the tongues started to wag around the Leicestershire village where she lived in so much style and comfort.

Some years after Lady Barnett's husband died in 1970, there was a suspicion among local shop-keepers that she was taking things without paying for them. No one could quite believe it, because although she was undoubtedly upset at the loss of Sir Geoffrey, she had put on a brave face and seemed to be getting on with her normal busy life, travelling all over the country to give lectures and after-dinner speeches. Even when it became clear that there was no mistake and that Lady Barnett was in fact shoplifting, there was a great deal of sympathy for her. For nearly two years, and despite the more malicious gossip, there was a local conspiracy to protect her from herself. Shopkeepers who saw her steal – always small, inexpensive items – simply added the cost to her bill and said nothing. She always paid without query. If she had any awareness that other people knew what was going on, she never gave any indication. The mask of coolness, carefully constructed over so many years, never slipped.

Shoplifting is, of course, not all that uncommon among well-to-do women just past middle age. There is a strong pattern that shows most of them are widowed or emotionally-neglected by their husbands and families, and some psychiatrists say that the thefts are often a thrilling escape from monotony and depression. Like most victims of this inexplicable syndrome,

Lady Barnett may well have overcome her problems in time, if she had not been titled and famous. But because she was, the local gossip gained wider circulation and when one of the shopkeepers decided that enough was enough and reported her to the police, the newspaper head-line writers had a field day. Today, people on pedestals are just sitting ducks.

No one, however, can be blamed for what happened next. Most people would have realized that the scandal – if scandal it was – would be just another nine-day wonder. But not Lady Barnett. As she saw it, her reputation was being destroyed and everything she had built up over the years was beginning to disintegrate. Her perceptions were, of course, clouded by her upbringing in a household – and in an age – where appearances were very important, where the paramount concern was what neighbours and friends might think. Her own ingrained sense of propriety, after her Presbyterian childhood and Quaker education, mitigated against any real understanding that the trauma would soon be over and that, in the end, people would think none the less of her because of the incident. Although she had lived happily in the public gaze and enjoyed the heady success of popularity for so many golden years, she must have felt unable to bear the knowledge that her indiscretions had been paraded so brutally in the mass media. She killed herself.

Because of her intensely private nature we shall never know how long she had been going through her private hell; but the public build-up to the tragedy began just before her sixty-second birthday in June 1980, when she was summoned to appear, later in the summer, before Loughborough magistrates on a charge of stealing a carton of cream and a tin of fish, valued at eighty-seven pence. This followed an incident earlier in the year, when she was questioned by the police about allegations made by one of the shopkeepers.

Lady Barnett told no one about the matter, and the first any of her family or friends knew about it was when they read it in the newspaper or heard it on radio. They were all very shocked; but, totally unaware of any anxiety or problems worrying her, they were also disbelieving. They all assumed that there had been a terrible mistake, some awful misunderstanding.

Mrs Jeanne Burton, Lady Barnett's secretary for fourteen years and co-director of her lecture agency, received the news secondhand, from her mother who had heard it on the local radio station: 'Of course I didn't believe it for a moment. Lady B had never said a word about any trouble and she had been her

3

usual cheerful self when she went off earlier that day for a lunch engagement in London.' Mrs Molly Cox, a lifelong friend – they had gone to the same schools in Glasgow and York – learned about it from another friend, Rosemary Anderson, who had seen it in the newspapers: 'Rosemary thought it might be true but I was certain it was all a mistake and that Isobel would explain it when I phoned her. This I did and she completely convinced me with her story.' Mrs Norah Cheatle, one of Lady Barnett's local friends in Leicestershire, says that when she spoke to her about the summons the day after it had been in the newspapers, she admitted that she had taken a couple of items from the local supermarket and that she had not paid for them: 'But she said she had been very muddled at the time and hadn't really known what she was doing. She obviously didn't need to steal and she said she certainly didn't mean to. It was all a mistake. She didn't seem unduly concerned and shrugged it off as just one of those things.' Mrs Cheatle, a friend for nearly thirty years, happily accepted that explanation and, for the time being at least, stopped worrying.

Lady Barnett herself carried on apparently as normal. Later in the same week she fulfilled two important speaking engagements and in each case showed all her usual wit and enthusiasm. She also carried on with all her social commitments – coffee with neighbours, dinner parties, and her regular series of bridge parties – with no indication that her sense of fun had in any way diminished. Only a car accident a fortnight later gives any real hint that the summons and the impending court case might have been preying on her mind. Two days before her birthday, she was driving home in the early evening when she crashed into a furniture van. Her car was a complete write-off, but she was lucky enough to escape serious injury, sustaining only bruised ribs, mild concussion and two black eyes. She told friends that the accident happened because she had been listening to the tennis from Wimbledon on her car radio. When the match finished, she leaned forward to change stations to find some music and somehow, at the same time, she had put her foot on the accelerator rather than the brake causing her to shoot across a junction and hit the van. Her car was a powerful BMW automatic which she usually drove very fast but expertly. She was a member of the Institute of Advanced Motorists and it was her first accident in forty years of driving.

Even after this incident, she seemed determined to carry on as normal. After the usual hospital checks, she went home and refused to bother the family doctor. Like so many medical people, she did not want anyone else poking into her state of health and tried to shrug it all off. Instead of going to bed, she sat down to write various letters including a thank-you note to Molly Cox:

My dear Molly,
You are wonderful to remember my birthday and this year it was even more marvellous. I had an almighty car accident on Saturday night – knocked unconscious and carted to the Leicester Royal Infirmary to make sure that I had not fractured my skull or broken anything and fortunately was allowed to leave and come home. What a birthday eve!

Lady Barnett and Mrs Cox had been writing to each other for nearly fifty years and this was one of the few letters not penned in her firm, stylish hand-writing. She explained it away with her usual wit: 'Apologies for this being typed but really my writing and concentration are nil and I wanted to get it off today in case I start having fits tomorrow!'

The next evening, Lady Barnett insisted on playing in a pre-arranged bridge match. Her partner was Mrs Cheatle: 'I had never seen her look so awful but she didn't want any sympathy – she never did – and we carried on playing throughout the evening, though I have to admit that on this occasion she was a simply dreadful partner.'

She only succumbed to medical treatment and firm instructions to do nothing but rest when a worried Mrs Burton contrived to get the family doctor to visit the house on another pretext. She was therefore able to ride out the worst effects of the delayed shock which hit her about ten days afterwards.

Two months later, when she appeared to be fully recovered from her injuries, Lady Barnett made the most astonishing decision of her life, and while it was obviously made under terrible pressures, it was a misjudgement that could only add to her anguish. She declined to appear before the local magistrates and elected instead to go for trial before a jury at Leicester Crown Court.

She had already admitted, to the police as well as to her friend Mrs Cheatle, that she had taken the items listed in the charge, without making any attempt to pay for them. The discovery of a large extra pocket sewn inside her coat suggested an intent to keep the items, so that, as a former magistrate herself, she must have known that she was at the very least technically guilty of theft. Under the circumstances, she could have been expected to plead guilty at the magistrates court and enter a statement in mitigation – an explantion offered in the hope of being dealt with leniently. She had sat in adjudication in dozens of similar cases and she must have known that the Bench is almost always very sympathetic to women they regard more as victims than offenders. It is probable that she would have been given a conditional discharge and quietly steered in the direction of appropriate medical help.

By electing to go to the Crown Court, she was subjecting herself to the ordeal of a full public trial, a painfully distressing experience whether one is guilty or innocent. Just what was in her mind when she made this decision? Was she under the delusion that she really was innocent and that the jury would say so to prevent her good name from being further besmirched? Or did she simply think that her tremendous popularity would sway the court into throwing out the case, saving her from the shame and humiliation of a conviction for stealing? Was she as irrational as she must have been when she went off shoplifting in the first place and therefore subconsciously looking for another thrilling escape from monotony and depression? Or was she cold-bloodedly trying to save face? Whatever she was thinking, she opted to take on the jury system in a gamble as wild as a game of Russian roulette and for stakes that proved to be every bit as high.

On Wednesday 15 October 1980, Lady Barnett, former Lady Mayoress of the city, ex-magistrate, widow of a much-respected solicitor and herself one of the Midlands' most distinguished citizens, found herself in the dock at Leicester Crown Court. For two long days she was forced to sit there in grim-faced silence while the prosecution carefully unfolded the evidence against her and her own counsel painstakingly examined the intimate detail of the case for the benefit of the jury. On the press benches, journalists from all the national newspapers, radio and television made hurried notes for the stories they would later relay to the now-fascinated public. At the end of the summing up, the jury filed out and Lady Barnett sat passively waiting while they deliberated. When they came back to deliver their verdict, she was visibly shaken and the judge was sympathetic: 'No sentence that I can pass can match the punishment you have already suffered by way of waiting for this trial and also, no doubt, the disgrace from this finding of guilty.' But he was also firm: 'People who enjoy public esteem and acclaim should set an example.' He fined her £75 and ordered her to pay prosecution costs of £200.

As she left the court, looking tired and drawn, she said she was shattered by the verdict and admitted that the trial had been a horrible experience and a considerable ordeal. Her awful gamble had failed and it was very much a loser's look that the photographers captured for the next day's newspapers.

The judge had been right, too, when he suggested that the punishment had started long before her actual court appearance. Her friends had seen the strain on her face soon after the initial publicity and, hard as she tried to cover up, the cracks began to show. She somehow lost her air of natural elegance. She wore the same stylish clothes as always, but indefinably they did not look the same on the days she lost her straight-backed upper-crust bearing. The arthritis which she normally ignored seemed to cause her terrible pain and whenever she did manage a smile, it looked forced.

The judge was not the only one who expressed sympathy. At her home, the telephone never stopped ringing and the postman delivered letters by the sackful. It was clear that at least some of the love and affection of her brightest days on television had survived the bitter test. Everyone who called or wrote expressed sympathy and offered good wishes for the future. Even the national press – obsessed as many of the reporters had been by the scandal potential of the story – was mainly generous in its commentary and several newspapers carried leading articles calling for a new and more understanding approach in these sorts of cases.

It looked as if the ordeal, self-inflicted as it might have been, was over – just another nine-day wonder. By the end of the week and with almost superhuman effort, Lady Barnett had forced herself back into some semblence of routine. Apart from a few awful moments at the end of the court hearing, she gave no outward sign of feeling sorry for herself. Under the circumstances, most people would have allowed themselves to wallow in self-pity, but such behaviour was anathema to her. Having readjusted her mask of coolness and having locked firmly in place her self-protecting shutters, she calmly applied herself to the task of replying personally to all the letters and messages. On the Saturday morning, she rang Mrs Cheatle and asked her round for coffee: 'Unfortunately I simply couldn't make it because I was feeling so ill myself after all the shock and worry of the court case. But Isobel was amazing. She was so cool and calm and talked cheerfully about going to play bridge later in

7

the afternoon. I was much more down than she was. She didn't seem the slightest bit depressed ... but then, of course, she wasn't the sort of person who would ever let on even if she was feeling low.'

She did play bridge on the Saturday afternoon and although there was a slightly strained atmosphere because some of those present simply were not sure whether or not to mention the trial, she seemed very much her old self.

Her son, Alastair, who had come back to live at the White House after his father's death in 1970, was away for the weekend and Lady Barnett spent the Sunday on her own. As usual, most of the morning went on reading the newspapers and listening to her old friend, David Jacobs, on the radio. In the afternoon she watered her hundreds of houseplants and chatted on the telephone to two or three other friends. Everything appeared quite normal.

The first sign that there might be something amiss came later in the evening when Mrs Audrey Green, who had been the daily help for the family for many years, noticed that the milk was still on the doorstep: 'I nearly rang to see if she was all right but in the end I decided not to disturb her because I thought she was probably having a good rest.' When Alastair returned much later, he made the same assumption and went straight to bed without seeing her.

On the Monday morning, Alastair could not hear any sound from her bedroom and spoke to Mrs Angela Stoneman, who had been the daily help for three years. She called the gardener, George Edmundson, and all three went upstairs to investigate. They saw steam coming from the bathroom and, inside, they found Lady Barnett dead in the bath.

As was later revealed at the inquest, she had taken a massive overdose of pain-killing tablets, more than double the normal lethal dose. The coroner said: 'She was a doctor and I cannot believe that suddenly, after all she had done in the past, she had made a stupid mistake and had taken an overdose of tablets by accident. I am satisfied she took the fatal dose deliberately.' Any lingering doubt about whether or not it was a mistake was removed by a close friend who recalled a discussion with Lady Barnett when they were both suffering from pain. Talking about safe dosages of drugs, she had said that the body's immune system was so stimulated by pain that it was possible for someone in agony safely to take an otherwise lethal amount of drugs such as morphia. If this was her understanding, and aware of her arthritis, she would have assumed that she needed to take considerably more than the amount required to kill someone else. By taking more than double the lethal dosage, she was being efficient to the very end.

It was her secretary, Mrs Burton, who seemed to sum up the shocked reaction to the tragedy: 'We are heartbroken. It is not believable. We all loved her so much and we all thought she was bearing up so well after the case.' And underlining Lady Barnett's apparent resilience, the coroner said: 'She appeared to have retained her dignity and charm and, right up to the time of her death, she appeared to be in complete control.'

It is never easy to offer a satisfactory explantion as to why anyone should take their own life. In this case it is even more difficult. All her fears that her friends and fans would be scandalized by the court case and either desert her or think badly of her were totally and demonstrably unfounded. She could not have had more evidence of people's sympathy, understanding and affection. Almost anyone else would have been overwhelmed by the warmth of the response, but for Lady Barnett it does not seem to have been enough.

Was it that her lifelong determination to stifle anxieties and keep up appearances had so damped down her own emotions that she could not read, or believe, the signs of genuine concern and love in other people? Or was it because her upbringing had instilled in her such high moral standards that – whatever anyone else might say – she could not bear to have fallen short in her own estimation?

Only Lady Barnett could provide the answers and there was some suggestion that she was planning to give an exclusive account of her problems to one newspaper. It was reported that she had agreed to talk to their reporter on the day she was found dead. Those who knew her best, however, all say that it is inconceivable that she could even contemplate such a soul-searing experience, and they point to her reluctance to discuss any of her worries, however minor, with even her closest friends. Her secretary, a meticulous guardian of her diary, says she can find no trace of an appointment. But even if there had been and it had been kept, it seems unlikely that even the shrewdest of Fleet Street's journalists could have inveigled the answers from the determinedly-private Lady Barnett.

One of her closest friends, Norah Cheatle, tried and failed. She now admits: 'Even after thirty years, I think I now have to say that I didn't really know Isobel. She really was a very private person.' But because she was *Lady* Barnett and because she was one of television's first superstars, there will be those who will go on trying to solve the enigma.

CHAPTER 2

*I*sobel Morag Marshall was very clearly one of those lucky people for whom the cliché about the silver spoon was coined. She was born at the tail-end of the First World War – on Sunday 30 June, 1918 – into a very comfortable, upper-middle-class, Scottish household largely unaffected by wartime privations. It was true that her father, a quiet, eminent Glasgow doctor, was still serving in the army in France, but her mother had all the security of the extended family and was able to go back to her parents' home in Aberdeen to be waited on hand and foot during this, her first confinement.

A few weeks after Isobel's birth, her mother went back to Glasgow – on the train, first class of course, with the baby snugly wrapped in a spare fur coat – to await the heroic return from France of Dr Marshall. The wait in the grimy, unhealthy atmosphere of the city was no less comfortable than in Aberdeen because the Marshalls were a big family – six brothers and sisters – and the uncles and aunts were always around to spoil the new baby and to make sure that she and her mother had absolutely everything they could possibly need. In the big house in Newton Place, food shortages and other wartime privations were unknown.

When he eventually arrived back from France after the armistice, Dr Marshall resumed his practice from the family home. Born a Victorian and having served in the army during the war, he was a stern disciplinarian – already into middle age, and set in his ways – who ruled his household firmly in the prevailing traditions of Scottish Presbyterianism. But he was also a shy, bookish man whose interests, other than medicine, were reading and listening to music. His library reflected his narrow taste in literature – rows of dry, historical tomes alongside his medical textbooks. He went to concerts at least twice a week, showing a much more catholic appreciation of music, with a hint of preference for Beethoven. Neither literature nor music, however, were allowed to interfere with his beloved profession. He was totally dedicated and never stopped studying. Medicine was a fast-developing field and to keep abreast of new discoveries and techniques, he read each learned paper as it was published and travelled all over Britain and Europe – no mean feat in those difficult days between the wars – to listen to lectures and to watch operations by the finest surgeons.

Mrs Marshall, the oldest of a family of ten, was as extrovert and gregarious as her husband was shy. Nor did she share his interests in books and music, although she did go to all the concerts with him out of her sense of wifely duty. She was an energetic, practical lady who was never happier than when supervising the running of the busy household and the even busier practice. She spent much of her time issuing instructions to the nanny and the housekeeper and the kitchen-maids, and when she was not checking up that everything was being done properly, she was helping to cope with the steady flow of patients.

There is no doubt that the whole household revolved around the good doctor and his patients. His specialism was neurology and there was a tacit acceptance that many of his visitors would be of a nervy disposition. He ruled, therefore, that the consulting-rooms should offer a quiet, calm sanctuary from the world outside. Mrs Marshall meekly accepted that a baby in a pram might just cry and so cause unnecessary anxiety in an onlooking patient, and as a consequence she saw nothing unreasonable in having to smuggle little Isobel in and out of the house by a back stairway.

Inevitably such restraint was to have its effect on Isobel as she grew up. She had inherited much of her mother's energy and zest, but because noise was not permitted during surgery hours, she had to repress her natural tendencies and save up her noisier games for Saturdays. Sundays, though also patient-free, were strictly-observed days of rest and religion.

Even Dr Marshall's love of music and his desire to stimulate a similar passion in his daughter was inhibited by the imagined needs of the patients. Isobel was roused from her bed just after six o'clock in the morning so that she could get in an hour's piano practice before the first visitor arrived. The tiny mite sat in the huge, draughty music-room trying to find the right notes with cold, stiff fingers while the fire in the tiny Victorian grate bravely warmed the chilly atmosphere degree by degree.

It is little wonder that the young Isobel often loathed her father's profession and his apparently demanding patients. She once recalled sitting at the top of the staircase watching the comings and goings and having desperately to resist an urge to throw heavy objects down on their heads. But it was long before she could blame the patients that Isobel earned the reputation of being something of an *enfant terrible*. As soon as she learned to walk, she also mastered the art of escaping, from both cot and nursery. She set a family record on one occasion when she made it all the way to the kitchen, down three flights of stairs and through three supposedly-closed, child-proof doors. There she discovered some wonderful new toys – a dozen freshly-laid eggs, delivered in a nice little basket only that morning. She managed to break every shell, eat most of the raw yolk and cover herself from head to toe in egg-white before being recaptured.

Less amusing was the time she bungled her escape at the first hurdle and was found hanging outside the cot with her head firmly trapped between the wooden slats. She was only saved by the power of her lungs and the noise she was able to generate. Even so, she was blue in the face by the time the luckless nanny came to the rescue. Only a few months later she again came close to precipitating her own demise and that of the rest of the household, having discovered matches. Playing with these magic sticks which burst into pretty colours whenever scratched against the box, she decided to experiment by seeing if she could transfer the colour to the white of the nursery curtains. It worked – so well that within seconds the flames spread and caused extensive damage. Luckily, the nanny was at that moment on her way back to the nursery and so disaster was averted. Baby Isobel was put under twenty-four-hour guard, with a second nurse drafted in to share the shifts and to spread the burden of constantly supervising the dangerous prisoner. And there is no doubt that that is how little Isobel saw herself. The atmosphere in the house was correct enough to satisfy any of its original Victorian occupants and life in the nursery was very much a life apart from the rest of the household. The room itself was well out of earshot of the other living rooms and there was a stern regime that made one day very much like another – up at the same time, bath at the same time. Even the menus had an awful sameness – 'lightly-boiled eggs, chicken-broth, milk pudding, steamed fish and bread and butter' – and each meal was consumed under the beady eye of nanny and the housekeeper.

The routine was broken only on Sundays, but even then it was only relaxed in favour of another equally-rigid programme – best clothes, special cake for tea, lectures on good manners, the privilege of having the companionship of a favourite doll and, whatever the weather, a long walk to church. Dr and Mrs Marshall were scrupulous in their observance of the Scottish Sabbath. The walk to church was not for the exercise, but because they would not use the car on God's own day. Newspapers were not allowed in the house because no one should be expected to work on a Sunday. Even knitting or sewing were positively frowned upon and anything as joyous as a noisy, childish game was totally forbidden. But young Isobel was, of course, unaware of all this as an unnatural discipline and she simply enjoyed her break from the monotony of the nursery.

Although there is no doubt that she was an exceptionally bright child, it was her father's status more than anything else which allowed her to go to school when she was only three, an unheard of privilege in the 1920s. The teachers might not have been so keen to pander to the well-connected Dr Marshall's whim if they had known what they were letting themselves in for. Having wrought havoc at home, she became a holy terror at school. Possibly as a reaction to the confinement of the nursery, she gave full reign to her phenomenal energy. She always ran when she should have walked; bumped into all and sundry, from the headmistress down; fell over twice a day; lost every hat she ever wore; made holes in every pair of stockings; and created panic in all the teachers.

No doubt the staff heaved a great sigh of relief when the bell went to mark the end of lessons. But while most of her friends then ran off to play for an hour or so, Isobel had to go home to parents determined to provide her with the best possible education and who had, therefore, thoughtfully employed a governess to give her extra tuition. Life to the little girl must at that stage have seemed an endless series of educational instruction: nature study, history, needlework – which she particularly disliked – art, music and geography. It was not the most exciting life for such a lively girl and she often shrugged off the tedium by escaping into a fantasy world, where grown-ups actually talked *to* her instead of *at* her. She found the entrance to this new world one night when her wretched loneliness at the top of the house became too much for her and she crept out of bed and downstairs to listen to the sounds of a dinner party. Soon she was enthralled by the conversation, and in her mind she was inside at the table, with everyone addressing her as an equal. It was a lovely feeling and she began to look forward to her vigil at the dining-room door.

She also discovered another world when, one night, her parents were out and she heard noises coming from the kitchen. She stole down the back stairs and listened at the door as the maids and some of their friends had an impromptu party of their own. Like many of the prominent Glasgow families, the Marshalls always took their servants from the Highlands, and most of them were Gaelic-speaking. That night Isobel could not understand a single word that was said, but she was enchanted by the lilting songs they sang together and from then on, she spent many hours crouched in the cold outside the kitchen, listening to the gay chatter interspersed with the sad, haunting melodies of the Highlands.

Isobel clearly had a closer affinity with the Highlands than she did with Glasgow and even as a child she relished the thought of holidays in Aberdeenshire, where her grandparents, aunts and uncles conspired to make her forget the privations of the city. Up there, there were ponies to ride, new lambs to feed, new-laid eggs to collect from the hen-coop. There were fewer stairs to climb, but just as many rooms to poke around in – the larder, with strange-looking birds hanging from hooks in the ceiling; the still-room, with hams soaking in brine, and whole sides of bacon; and the linen room, cool and fresh with the scent of dried lavender and rose petals. Even going to church seemed less of a duty. There was no need to walk; it was quite permissible to go by carriage, which was clearly not such an evil contraption as the motor car. And the sermon was made more tolerable by the surreptitious sucking of sweets, which had earlier been handed out by a thoughtful uncle.

Those early holidays were always dominated by Isobel's maternal grandparents. Her grandfather was a gentle Highlander, with a long, flowing white beard, whose idea of discipline was to perch the little girl on his knee and tell her stories about the farm animals. Grandmother was different. She looked as if she had modelled herself on the late Queen, and was always regally dressed in black silk. She was the matriarch and the disciplinarian. With her own spine as straight as a rod, she was always admonishing Isobel to stand up straight. One day she told her: 'Walk as if you own the world and not as if you were Atlas trying to carry the burden on your shoulders.' It was a piece of advice the young girl never forgot.

Back in Glasgow, the six-year old Isobel found her routine

dramatically interrupted by the arrival of a new baby, her little brother Ian. She was suffering from whooping-cough at the time of his birth and instead of getting the fuss and attention that such an illness seemingly entitled one to, she was banished to suffer alone in the country, looked after by an aunt instead of her mother. However, she made up for such unfairness by almost ruining the Christening service, telling everyone, in a loud voice, how ugly the new baby looked and how she certainly would not play with such a shapeless bundle.

In fact, she did not have much chance to play with him. What Isobel, in her innocence, did not realize was that her childish perception was cruelly and unnervingly accurate. The child had been born with brain damage and as well as having a slight physical deformity, he was also mentally sub-normal. It is one of the darker sides of life in those days that such a child should be thought to bring shame on the family. To the modern and possibly more-enlightened mind, it seems impossible that anyone, let alone a highly intelligent, distinguished doctor, should attach stigma to mental disorder. Sadly, however, the Marshalls were prisoners of their day and they shrank from the responsibility of bringing the child up in their home. They followed grim custom and sent the little boy away, although not to one of the awful public institutions but to a private home, where he was to live out his blessedly-short life.

No one seems to know quite what was wrong with him nor even exactly when he died, although it is thought to be in the mid-1930s, when he would have been ten or eleven years old. Dr and Mrs Marshall appear to have been so distressed by their son's condition that once he had gone away they never discussed him with anyone. Nor do we know how Isobel felt about this episode, because she was drawn, unwittingly in the first place, into the family's conspiracy of shamed silence. One of her school friends can recall her writing to Ian, but she never spoke about him in any detail. Even many years later, when she published her autobiography in 1956, she left the cloak of secrecy very firmly in place. She mentioned her brother only in passing and made no comment about his illness, saying only that he died 'in childhood'. We therefore have no way of knowing how she felt about it in retrospect, as she herself moved into more enlightened times.

At the time, of course, she was young enough for the tragedy of the situation to pass over her head and it was a case of out of sight, out of mind. Her life proceeded as if nothing untoward had happened. At school, she was beginning to enjoy her lessons. The headmistress was a progressive educationalist and did not believe in either examinations or homework. Once they had mastered the three Rs, the pupils were given a fair amount of freedom to pace themselves against a syllabus that was set each month. Some girls might have taken liberties with such freedom, but not Isobel. She studied hard at school and then took work home because she enjoyed it so much. She even carried this enthusiasm with her when, at the age of eleven, she went on to a more orthodox girl's private school and had to face all the usual exams and compulsory homework. By then she had learned just how much it pleased her father to see her doing so well and, in her own words, she became like a thirsty sponge. She seemed to soak up each new item of knowledge with relish and she actually enjoyed the competitive tension that surrounded the exams. It is also true to say that she particularly enjoyed hearing the results, because she always did so well and was never out of the prize-list. She was beginning to develop the instinctive style of the winner.

She was not an especially sporty girl, mainly because her father had always railed against the 'jolly-hockeysticks brigade', convinced that such a game produced a special breed of Amazons. But she was keen on riding and swimming – pursuits she had first taken up during holidays in Aberdeenshire – and she was good at both.

It was an early taste of competitive swimming that caused the first cloud to appear on the horizon of Isobel's childish naïvety. It was a handicap race swum in heats and the handicaps were based on times achieved during the preliminaries. When it came to the final, Isobel was surprised to find that one of the girls who swam as well as she did had a long advantage over everyone else. Of course, she won the race easily, and then admitted that her mother had given her the tip not to swim her best in the heats in order to get the best handicap for the final. Isobel was outraged, not just because she felt the girl had cheated but also because it gave her a glimpse of how unfair life could be.

When they were not visiting relatives, the Marshalls' holiday was usually a two-month stay in a house somewhere in the Highlands or on one of the islands on the West Coast of Scotland. The preparations for such an adventure were spectacular. Trunks were packed with linen and silver; crates of food arrived from Glasgow's best grocer; and an extra cook was employed for the duration of the holiday. All the bodies, all the

17

provisions, all the luggage were carefully packed into two taxis, decanted into a first-class compartment on the train and then, after the long, relaxing journey, transferred into more taxis for the final, exciting leg of the expedition. Dr Marshall was never able to stay for the whole holiday, but more often than not cousins, aunts and uncles turned up to share the house and it was with them that Isobel learned to sail and to fish and even, small as she was, to shoot. Those were the idyllic days of her childhood and she enjoyed every moment of them. When one looks at the family album, at the pictures of carefree children and elegantly dressed adults, it is difficult to accept that they were taken against the drab backcloth of one of the grimmest periods of social unrest and economic gloom. In Britain there had been the 1926 General Strike and the hunger marches. In America three years later, there was the Wall Street crash. And in Glasgow in particular, unemployment and poverty were rife. But it was to be several more years before such conditions were to have repercussions on the successful doctor's family.

CHAPTER 3

Just as she was blissfully unaware of the adult world's terrible economic problems, so, in 1931, the young Isobel had not the faintest idea that long, serious discussions about her education were taking place between her parents. Her father had become more and more anxious about the social troubles flowing from the various crises that had split the Labour Government and forced Ramsay Macdonald to form a coalition in a desperate bid for some kind of national unity. The grim, unhealthily violent atmosphere of Glasgow was not the environment in which he wanted to see his only daughter grow up. He was aware that he would not be able to cocoon her from reality forever, but at least he could delay the inevitable as long as possible by sending her away to boarding school. Her mother was less keen on the idea. It was not all that usual for Scottish girls to leave home and she would certainly have preferred to keep Isobel under her own wing. Not surprisingly for the period, the child was never invited to comment. Even less surprisingly, it was Dr Marshall's view that prevailed and in the middle of the long, delightful summer holidays, Isobel learned with surprise that instead of going back to her old school in Glasgow in the autumn, she would be going to England, to the Mount School at York.

Her arrival at the Mount marked the beginning of one of the most important chapters in her life. Away from home and family for the first time and, at thirteen, still highly impressionable, she came under new influences that were to have a long-lasting effect on her.

The school itself was a beautiful place, a collection of lovely old buildings set amid sprawling acres of playing-fields, neatly-trimmed lawns and colourful flowerbeds – a far cry from the urban grime of the crowded city of Glasgow. It was run by the Society of Friends – the Quakers – and it was anything but a typical educational institution. The teachers were liberal in their approach to the task of preparing their young charges for the adult world. While they quite firmly demurred from the all-too-common assumption that academic training is somehow less important to girls than it is to boys, they also pursued the policy of building on whatever it was that each girl might be good at, whether it be Latin or ludo, history or hockey. It was, of course, easier for them to give this individual attention because there were only a hundred pupils in the school altogether.

When she first arrived, it was quickly evident that Isobel's Scottish education – reinforced, of course, by the attention of her personal governess – had put her academically in advance of the other girls in her age group, and as a result she did very little work in her first year. But while she was marking time in the classroom, she took the opportunity to read more outside the lessons. She had been a keen reader for many years, but nothing caught her girlish imagination quite like the novels of Jane Austen which she now discovered. Isobel with her nose in a book was to be a familiar sight throughout her life.

If she was marking time in the classroom, however, she was learning quite a lot about life in general. There were only the minimum of rules to regulate the confined community and once she realized these were for the benefit of the pupils as much as for the staff, Isobel slowly became more ready to exercize self-discipline than she had ever been before. Later, perhaps to her cost this was to become almost second nature to her and she used her training to screen her feelings from the world.

What she was not aware of at the time but did appreciate later was that each of the school's various customs and traditions were simply designed to help the girls assimilate more comfortably into the outside world. The importance of good manners, for example, was underlined by what to the girls then seemed like a most peculiar restriction. It manifested itself in the dining-room where it was positively forbidden for any girl to ask for anything – food, condiments, cutlery, even a glass of water – for themselves. Instead they were persuaded to the view that it was more Christian to be concerned with other people's well-being and each child was therefore expected to look after her neighbour's needs and wants. It meant, of course, that if no one passed the salt, food had to be eaten without it. There were two ways of surviving. The preferred way was to become such a good hostess that everyone else responded to your hospitality in a like manner. The alternative was that you became adept at manipulating friends with hints on the scale of discreet to heavy.

Isobel's natural instincts put her quickly into the good hostess category, but she never really mastered the rules of the second element of the game and she admitted later that throughout her life she spoiled meals by not being able to ask someone to pass the salt!

It was at the same dining-table that she learned one of the other social graces that was to stand her in such good stead in her later life – the art of conversation. She was to be forever grateful for the school's odd-sounding custom of 'sides'. The 'sides' were simply the neighbours one sat alongside on occasions such as mealtimes. Rather than allow the girls to develop unhealthy little cliques which invariably left the less personable girls out in the cold, the teachers allocated 'sides' on a strict rota basis so that no two girls sat by each other for any length of time. This had the bonus effect of teaching them how to establish at least basic relationships quickly and easily, because if they did not start chatting more or less instantly, they never really got to be friends with anyone. Isobel, always anxious to be liked by everyone and keen to be involved in whatever was going on, quickly established herself as a lively, chatty companion who was always popular with her randomly-chosen 'sides'. It was, perhaps, her success here that helped create her concern for what other people thought. Clearly if they thought highly of her, she would always have a 'side'.

Isobel was learning other things too. It was the Quakers' policy to take overseas pupils and while she was at the Mount, her horizons were considerably widened by rubbing shoulders with girls from China, Africa, America and several European countries; and it was through their missionary fund-raising activities that her social conscience was awakened, giving her a genuine concern for other people. But, perhaps most important of all, it was at this school that she learned the value of friends, and in her four years at the Mount she established several relationships that remained firm throughout her life.

One of these close friendships began when she was asked to look after another Glasgow girl who was a year younger and who was making the same switch from the city school to the Mount just as Isobel was moving up to the second year there. The girl was Molly Spencer (later to become Mrs Cox) and her mother had asked if Isobel might look after her on the long train journey to York. Although she was quite friendly on the way to the school, Isobel all but abandoned the younger girl once she was back among her friends. 'My mother had warned me that

21

Isobel would probably look after me well on the train,' recalls Mrs Cox, 'but that she might forget me when we arrived at the Mount. When she did, I remember wondering how on earth my mother had guessed!' But the system of 'sides' had yet another side-effect and that was to break down the age barriers that more usually kept teenage girls in separate peer groups. Slowly, therefore, the two young Scots became close friends.

Their friendship is traced in a remarkable collection of letters written over a period of nearly fifty years by Isobel to Molly. Initially they were kept for no other reason than that Mrs Cox was always reluctant to throw away such strong, personal reminders of her youth. Now, however, they represent an intriguing documentary on a privileged lifestyle and provide a wonderful insight into Lady Barnett's development from bubbling adolescence to graceful maturity. They also expose some of her weaknesses and underline many of her strengths.

The correspondence began in 1933, when Molly was in the school's sick bay, and the first note is hurredly written in a girlish scrawl on a scrap of paper torn from an exercise book:

Chère Molly,
This is being scribbled in French, We have just been given back those awful French dictées that we had, and this is my corrections!!
   I have to cave!! every min as LW wanders here occasionally.
   Well life is not so bad. Que possey-vous d'aller d'lécole. Nous nous missons you. Which room are you in? Big one?
   Well no more news. But buck up & get well.

                    Love
                    Isobel.

It might not be a particularly significant note but it was a great comfort to the sick girl, who was, of course, blissfully unconcerned by the shaky punctuation and the awful franglais. To her it meant that someone cared. It also shows that however she might have covered it up in public, the young Isobel really was quite thoughtful. At that time it was the style among some of the girls at the school to effect a rather blasé, almost cynical attitude to life. Indeed, the bloom was beginning to fade from Isobel's popularity and she was earning an unenviable reputation for having a waspish, cutting tongue. Among those she regarded as her equals, she indulged in constant verbal sparring and her vocabulary of cruel words usually gave her the upper hand. She was crushingly sarcastic and reduced many of the other girls to tears before she discovered that sarcasm is the lowest form of wit.

Another letter, written to Molly just after she had been made a prefect, again shows the thoughtfulness under the youthful, casual veneer:

Dearest Molly,
Knowing your fads so well, I know you don't eat chocolate and I know you haven't time to eat fruit, so I've sent you some of both, tho' you're a beastly nuisance.

I've also sent you a bottle of Lavender Water to soothe away the wrinkles & headaches of your office.

Now I'm going so

Cheerio
Isobel.

Letter writing was another of the social graces that young ladies were expected to acquire and Isobel quickly developed it into a fine art, penning notes to all and sundry at the slightest excuse. When she went home to Glasgow for the school holiday, she kept Molly up to date with her activities:

I have not actually been away. We were up at Peebles Hydro for two days and today I have just come back from a long motor run to Largs. We left early in the morning (ie about 11) and had lunch at a hotel. It was right up on a hill and from the lounge you got a heavenly view of Arran with snow-capped peaks and the Little Cumrie. You couldn't see Largs for trees, which was a dashed good thing.

On returning to school after that break, Isobel's youthful reverie was shattered when her father had a stroke and was left paralysed all down his right side. She was, however, spared the full horror of his condition for by the time she went home again he had, with astonishing determination, taught himself to write with his left hand and was beginning to walk again without assistance. When he died later in the year, the news was broken to her in such a roundabout way that she later said it came more as a relief than a shock. Because of his illness, she had been spending most of the summer holidays with some friends when an aunt suddenly arrived on the doorstep to take her home. There was no explanation offered and the journey to Glasgow was endured in uncomfortable silence. When the car that was waiting for them at the station then whisked them past the house to that of another aunt, poor Isobel was beside herself with fear and her anguish was added to by the tears and whispers that greeted her arrival. When someone plucked up the courage to tell her what happened, she wept in relief first and grief only later.

Her mother's resilience over the next few weeks provided Isobel with her first real lesson in maintaining a good front. She knew how close her parents had been, but never once did she see her mother crack, nor was there any suggestion that Isobel might have to leave school and return to live at home, despite the fact that Dr Marshall's death had considerably reduced the family's income. For the first time, in fact, it looked as if young Isobel might not be so well insulated from the realities of life in the 1930s. Because of the economic depression, all her father's stocks and shares were sold at rock-bottom prices and the resulting cash converted into securities to provide a regular but very much reduced income for Mrs Marshall and her daughter. They were far from being poor, but money was enough of a problem for there to be a large question-mark over Isobel's school fees. Against all advice, and despite the fact that it would have eased her own loneliness, her mother refused to take her away from boarding school and chose instead to make her own sacrifices.

Young Isobel was only vaguely aware of all this at the time, and when she went back to school she quickly put all the traumas behind her and settled down once more to enjoy life there. Her sharp tongue had not improved a great deal, nor was its application limited to the girls; some of the staff clearly suffered from her apparent contempt when she doubted their ability, and this was reflected in her end of term reports. In another letter to her friend Molly, she wrote:

I got quite a good report except from our dear Madelaine [the chemistry teacher who also took Isobel for scripture lessons]. She said I could be more helpful etc, etc. Now who on earth wants to help Madelaine in Scripture. I ask you!!!!! She gets in a big enough mess as it is without anyone getting her in a worse one, and if you start to help her in chemistry, well she asks you to take the class!! And then for my chemie and scripture reports she puts might be more helpful!!! Henceforth I sit in the front row.

But the bad report obviously had a sobering effect on her and in the same letter she asks for her friend's help:

Will you give me a side in chemistry? [Older girls were sometimes allowed to choose their own neighbours in class]. I'll promise to be good, and will you also give me one in Latin and Bilge [botany and

24

zoology]? You know I will be good and you'll have to use your good, steadying influence on me . . . please, Molly.

Like every girl of her age, Isobel often allowed herself to be side-tracked from the academic path and developed girlish crushes on some of her friends. Euphoric from a set of very good exam results, she wrote to Molly:

Another reason to hasten my insanity is that I've seen Elinor [an older girl at the Mount] just lately. She is over from Ireland staying with Morna and I've rediscovered how marvellous she is, and if ever anyone thought I was smut on Kate, tell them they're MAD. I like Elinor far, far, far better than Kate. Therefore I can't be smut on Kate. QED.

Isobel later described her school career as 'normal and undistinguished', although in fact she did well at most things. She had no difficulties in staying towards the top of her class academically; she became a prefect; and, despite her father's oft-expressed fears about Amazons, she gained her colours for hockey, cricket, swimming and gymnastics.

When the time came for long-term decisions about choice of careers, Isobel was never in any doubt. She wanted to follow her father's profession and planned to go to medical school. If her father had still been alive, things might not have gone that way. He had been very much against such an idea and had always tried to discourage her, pointing out how frustrating life was for women doctors because their real talents were seldom recognised by the male-dominated medical establishment. His opposition, added to her teachers' advice that her aptitude was more for the arts, and a self-awareness of her short-comings in mathematics would have been too much for even the determined Isobel to overcome. As it was, she did get her own way. All the surviving opponents succumbed to her single-mindedness.

Suspecting that he would try to prove she would never make a doctor, she refused point blank to subject herself to the psychologist brought in to give career advice. She said she knew her own capabilities and needs much better than he could possibly determine with his funny tests and obtuse questions. She tempered this youthful arrogance by acknowledging her maths problem and readily agreed to concentrate on that subject during the rest of her time at school.

Convinced that as a doctor's daughter, she had a near-inalienable right to go into medicine, Isobel decided she would go to Cambridge University. There is little doubt that her ability would have secured her a place there, but just then money problems arose once more and clouded the future. It soon became apparent that even with the help of a scholarship from the Quakers, it was unlikely that she would be able to stay on at the Mount until she was eighteen and even if she did, there was no hope of her mother being able to subsidise her years at Cambridge.

Eventually after a great deal of heart-searching and not a little judicious string-pulling by some of her father's former colleagues, it was agreed that she should leave school a year early and go to Glasgow University, where a place would be found for her in the medical school, even though she would still be only seventeen, and where she would be able to live at home without any extra expenses.

It was a masterly compromise, but neither that nor the short spell she had at a Swiss finishing school by way of compensation eased Isobel's sadness at having to leave all her friends in York. From a holiday cottage on the Isle of Arran, after she had just visited one of her best friends, she wrote to Molly Spencer:

I hated leaving her because now I have the awful feeling that no matter how often we write, or how often we see each other, we'll never be quite the same again. I never realised that I'd like anyone quite so much, and it makes me frightfully fed up at leaving school. Of course I'm feeling in a horribly morbid mood and when people say 'Oh but think of all the nice friends you'll meet at university,' I could murder them!

It was also a time for self-assessment and in the same long letter, Isobel apologized for her behaviour at school:

You really are the most marvellous person to tell things to because you're always so patient. How you do it I don't know but I always wanted to be like you in the way of being patient. I always wanted to get to know you better, but in lessons I always loved teasing you just to see if I could get you to be angry with me.

Then, after a little gossip about her current boyfriend, she added:

It's rather nice to be able to gabble on and on but you will tell me if you object because strange to say, I've just realised what a selfish person I am. But I don't suppose much can be done about it.

This same letter, like some of the others, hints at the insecurity that lay behind her cool exterior, especially in the postcript in which she wrote of her anxiety that no one should discover what 'an ass' she sometimes was. That afterthought was her first expression of fear that others might think badly of her, a fear that was to haunt her throughout her life.

CHAPTER 4

When Isobel arrived at Glasgow University, in October 1935, she was one of only nineteen girls among more than two hundred first-year medical school students, and it did not take her very long to learn why her father's lack of enthusiasm for her decision to become a doctor had turned to positive obstructiveness. There were a number of eminent men there who did not welcome the intrusion of females into their closed society. At one of the early lectures, the professor, distinguished but crotchety, surveyed the small band of girls grouped before him and sniped: 'Now I know why there is a shortage of domestic servants.' Luckily for Isobel, his antipathy was not shared by all his colleagues, for she was finding it difficult enough in any case to make the transition from carefree schoolgirl to responsible young adult. Her upbringing had been so sheltered that when she had to pay her fees to the university, it was the first time she had had anything to do with finances and she was not sure how to make out the cheque. But her education and breeding had also equipped her with a rock-solid base of self-confidence and determination. For her, new experiences were to be welcomed and enjoyed; problems were simply to be overcome. The professor's remark only made her all the more resolved to do well – to prove her father and all the other sceptics wrong. She had already confounded the doubters at her school by struggling through the dreaded maths exams with perfectly respectable pass marks. Now she would show this professor and his kind just of what Dr Marshall's little girl was made.

Her resolution was considerably strengthened by the advice she was getting from her fast-maturing friend Molly, and she showed her appreciation in a long letter written soon after she started at university:

My Dear Old Girl,

Just to thank you ever so much for your lovely long letter. I know how busy you are so that made it extra nice to receive such a nice letter from you. It didn't offend me in the least, after all I had asked for your advice, and I was only too glad to get it. I've always had a large chunk of admiration for your advice altho' I didn't always like to admit it!

I really will try to follow your advice about the smiling, altho' Margaret [Isobel's closest school friend] was always telling me that I shouldn't smile such a wide smile as it only showed what a collosal mouth I have. Never mind I'll show everyone all my teeth, and I expect it will be slightly easier to keep my temper at Varsity because I'll never come into such close contact with the Varsity people as I did with all my Mount School friends. The only reason that Margaret and I managed to live together was because of Margaret's tact and patience. I think she might be slightly rewarded by knowing that it was mainly due to her friendship that I had such a heavenly last year. I daren't tell her so because I always put things so badly in letters.

No, I can definitely state on irrevocable evidence that you are not a prig! Otherwise I shouldn't be writing to you now. I always have a nasty feeling in the pit of my somewhat protruding tum-tum when I'm in the presence of a prig and I haven't experienced said feeling while in your presence.

About using my friends. Yes I suppose I did. I never really thought of it like that, but I know I used to get ever so annoyed with Margaret over nothing, and I always had an uncomfy feeling deep down that I was a nasty cat but I resolutely squashed the said feeling. You see I really did like Margaret immensely and being rather selfish I was frightened that she'd like other people better than me.

After acknowledging what were obviously a few home truths, she seemed none too sure about her new life:

I can't give you my impressions of a university because they're awfully hazy. It's fun however and people are awfully kind in telling you where to go because as the place is so collosal you get completely lost. I'm rather scared of things and people but on the whole I think I'll love it – in time!

At seventeen, she was the youngest girl in the University, and she was bombarded with invitations to join almost every society and group on the campus. Most teenagers would have been tempted by so much flattering attention, but Isobel knew how easy it would be to fail and she was totally committed to finishing with a good degree. It was, of course, easier for her to resist temptation because she lived at home and was able to escape from the University fairly quickly at the end of lectures. She might have been more tempted to stay and take part if she had had to share digs – often of a very uncomfortable nature – like most of her fellow-students. Typically, however, she remained sheltered from such problems. Although not so well off as when Dr Marshall was alive, the family were still comfortable and when elderly relatives died, Isobel invariably received a bequest in their wills. She was always able to spend the money on herself. She bought a lot of clothes and was usually the neatest, best-dressed of the younger students. But although she also used some of the money for travelling, including a Mediterranean cruise, it would be a mistake to assume she was unduly extravagant. In fact, she always handled her money very well, and with an ability inherited from generations of canny Scots, she was careful never to settle for less than full value for her pounds.

It was, of course, the fact that she had money to be careful with that underlined her insulation from reality. Following her father's death and the consequent re-organization of the family's finances, she was aware that the country had been going through very difficult times, but, with Stanley Baldwin restored as Tory Prime Minister for a third and record term, life in her social set went on very much as before, and in January 1936 she wrote again to her friend, Molly:

I've been at stacks of dances, there seem to have been more than ever this year. Mary Craddock's was especially nice tho' the ages ranged from 8 to 28. I got a small boy aged eight and a half in a Paul Jones. He confided to me that he's taken dancing lessons, but I waltzed differently from the way he waltzed but however he didn't mind doing my waltz! The perfect gentleman eh what? 8½!'

This was all part of the gay whirl that was known as the season and later in the year, when she was eighteen, it was Isobel's turn to 'come out' as one of Scotland's brightest debutantes.

Anyone who lived in Glasgow at the time, or who read about it in books like *No Mean City*, will find it hard to believe that there could have been a season in those grim days of 1936. In their book – described at the time as 'the most outspoken novel of the century' – Alex McArthur and Kingsley Long paint a terrible picture of dirt, drink, poverty and brutality and although they were writing about the notorious Gorbals, the atmosphere of fear and violence permeated the whole of Glasgow and, indeed, some of the nearby towns like Paisley and Greenock. Against such a backcloth, Scotland's gay young things wrapped themselves in the finest silks and satins for a merry-go-round of parties and balls in which parents tried to outdo each other in the lavishness of their hospitality as they presented their daughters to a society gasping for new marriage-fodder. At five feet ten inches, tall and stunningly-attractive, Isobel was one of the undoubted successes of the season and simply revelled in all the attention and flattery. She was invited to most of the dances and, in between, was a guest at many of the city's great houses, witnessing the high life at close quarters.

For her second year at medical school, she was to concentrate on anatomy and physiology and rather than waste money on new books, she decided to raid her father's library, rescuing from the dust his well-used copy of *Gray's Anatomy*. From a cupboard, she also unearthed the old skeleton he had used some fifty years earlier during his own student days. There was a special thrill for her in using her father's things, and she was so proud to be following in his footsteps that it took her several months to find out just how far medical knowledge had advanced in half a century. A couple of generations of experts had discovered various bits and pieces of the human body that neither the good Mr Gray nor the man who had assembled the old skeleton knew existed. While her knowledge of anatomy would have allowed her to sail comfortably through the stiffest of exams in 1878, there were too many gaps for 1936.

In working twice as hard to fill in these holes, Isobel also began to close the gap between her perceptions and the reality of life. Her first step was in the anatomy room where, like most of her fellow students, she was confronted by death for the first time. She had known it was coming because the medical tutors had spent some time trying to prepare the young students for their introduction to a cadaver. The tutors, of course, had taken much delight in building up a chamber-of-horrors atmosphere, and the students were suitably subdued as they trailed along dusty corridors, down an old spiral staircase, through the poorly-lit museum with its strange bottles of anatomical specimens and then, suddenly, back into incredibly bright lights and sweet smells – the overhead arcs and the formaldehyde of the dissecting room. Isobel had been warned that she might well faint at her first sight of the bodies and when she didn't, she was so relieved that she almost laughed out loud. In her next letter to Molly Spencer, she wrote:

Though my knees were clacking together in grand style before I went into the place, as soon as I got in I didn't mind a bit as they don't look like people at all. They look rather like Red Indians with masks on, and you don't feel as if you're dealing with humans at all.

She never again suffered from the irrational fear of dead bodies and she said that it was her anatomy sessions that helped her to accept death as a perfectly natural phenomenon rather than some great, spiritual disaster. Certainly she seemed to take the gory classes in her stride:

The swots think I'm an imbecile heading for the local loony bin merely because I introduce a spot of cheerful jazz into anatomy. I merely sing the Hallelujah Chorus over the body and they all shake their heads and make noises like a flock of agitated hens. The bright young things on the other hand seem to think I'm not bright enough, merely because I don't choose to miss an average of five lectures per week. Gosh how I long for a Mount School-ite with a sensible outlook somewhere between the two. The swots seem to think that 'cos you sing you can't work so this morning, I reeled off to three of them, one and a half pages of our anatomy book – verbatim! Gad, you'd have been quite weak if you'd seen their faces! It bucked me up no end.

Isobel clearly enjoyed correcting any mistaken impressions, especially about her ability, and she was therefore doubly excited when the results of the first year's exams were announced and she could write to Molly:

Oh I must tell you my exam results because I'm so proud of them!! Out of our class of 200 nitwits – I was 2nd in Materia Medica (drugs, pills, prescriptions etc) beaten only by a man who has been a chemist for 15 years! In surgery I was 4th so I am feeling definitely among the high up ones. Gosh but it does make me horribly unpopular among the women! Because I have been to every big medical and university dance this term (Oct – Dec – 23 dances in all) they get the impression that I don't work – which I do like blazes. Then the more unpleasant females actually as good as told me that I wouldn't do well, and it was common talk that Isobel was one of those awfully gay girls. Now they are madder than ever because I've beaten them all by miles!!!!! They harbour a grudge 'cos they think they worked harder than I did – bosh – they don't know how to work that's all.

It was perhaps just as well that Isobel had also been working equally hard on her sharp tongue by holding back on her more caustic comments and with some success:

Do you know Molly, I'm getting awfully good at not losing my temper! You see I haven't got time to lose it!! We have one lecture and then an absolute scrum and then another lecture, more scrum etc. etc. so I'm too busy collecting my belongings and jabbering to people to remember that I've got a temper. Things are looking up.

Despite her temper and what to many of them must have seemed like an obsession for her profession, Isobel was very popular with the young men and her attendance at twenty-three dances in three months is ample evidence that she very much enjoyed their attentions. She had many admirers, not just in the medical school or the university, but somehow she managed to keep them all at arm's-length. Referring to one who thought he was special to her, she wrote:

I like him a lot. He's a sport and really awfully nice, but then I think I like at least six other boys like that. They do make such marvellous friends and at the moment I don't want any more so I don't expect they do either.

Of another friend who seemed to be getting too involved, she said: 'It's shameful. She's turning into a brazen hussy and she ought to be smacked!' The language of that note perfectly underlines the moral tone of the period.

At eighteen, Isobel seemed to prefer older men and she even looked at the professors with more than a scholarly eye:

Prof really is a most attractive man and it's a scream to watch the maiden hearts, seated in the front row, give an unmaidenly flutter when the said hero ambles in. For once I am not smitten, however. He rather annoys me because he's got an untidy mind and his notes are a bit rambly. I long to take him in hand. You know, teach him to underline his headings in red ink and put all dates in the margin.

Disconcerted by the professor's untidy mind, she concentrated her attentions on a twenty-eight-year-old doctor who, as a postgraduate student, was still of a clinically logical bent. She told Molly how much she liked him:

A young doctor for whom I have a great admiration holds forth that woman should be a domesticated animal and so heigh-ho Isobel sets out to conquer domesticity! Result being that the household is suffering from a superfluity of burnt offerings. Mum is developing a digestion like an ostrich and if I don't stop soon, we'll lose our maids, which are as a couple of pearls without price. Here endeth the domesticity! Imagine liking a man ten years older than myself, who probably has half a dozen women after him. Just tell me how absolutely cracked I am, and I know it, but it does me good to be told!

She wasn't too far out in her estimation of the man's fidelity. They went out together every Tuesday and Saturday and Isobel concentrated her studies on her other evenings, assuming he was doing the same. He was not. He was courting another girl student on Mondays and Thursdays and a third on Wednesdays and Fridays. Presumably he rested on Sundays. The discovery of his faithlessness did little damage to Isobel's teenage heart, but the blow to a fragile ego was enough for her to register that charming people were not always as straight-forward as they seemed. Another layer of naivety had been peeled away.

CHAPTER 5

*F*ew of her fellow students, and none of her tutors, could have guessed that Isobel ever suffered from insecurity or self-doubt. What they saw was a lively, highly-intelligent young lady who, if anything, was a touch over-confident. She seemed to know exactly where she wanted to go and was striding boldly along her chosen career-path with commendable single-mindedness. Even the dreaded exams, which brought most young medics to their knees, held no terror for her. She boasted of a photographic memory which, she said, allowed her to visualize the appropriate page of any textbook at will and made most of the papers easy for her to complete. Underneath all the bravado, however, there was an insecure teenager trying to get out and when the subject she had not enjoyed at school – physics – tripped her up again, she was very upset. When she failed her oral examination and was told she would have to take it again the following year, she poured her heart out to her one confidante, Molly Spencer, saying she wished she was back at the Mount:

I loved not having to worry about things, everything was arranged for
you, and you knew just what to do . . . At times I'm haunted by an
awful dread that I've probably chosen quite the wrong profession. I'm
not good with my hands – I can't be a surgeon. I've got the kind of brain,
that learns easily but doesn't observe much for itself. I won't make a
good diagnostician and lastly I haven't got the bed-side manner! There,
now you know why I'll never be a doctor and I must say it worries me a
lot when I think about it.

All this, of course, was just one of the symptoms of a young girl painfully discovering that growing up was not quite as easy as it looked. Only time and experience would solve the problems and certainly the next year she took a major step towards maturity when she had her first proposal:

It thrilled me frightfully, and yet frightened me a lot. The boy is about 28 and is a partner in his father's shipping firm. I've seen a lot of him ever since I left school. Most of the boys I know are all at varsity like myself. They have their careers to think of and can't get married for ages. Going about with them, one is quite safe as regards matrimony and it came as a fearful shock to me to think that this boy wanted to marry me. He is a dear and I like him tremendously but I don't think as yet I know the meaning of the word love. I feel so young and inexperienced and the thought that anyone could want to marry me gave me rather a jolt. Of course like most people (female) I have always vaguely thought I'd like to get married but the prospect seemed far away in the future. I adore babies and would love to have some of my own, but the thought of settling down and doing it straight away scared me. I don't think I can love him if the thought of giving up my medicine appals me so. Surely if one loves someone everything else will seem unimportant beside it?

Never never again Molly do I want to have a proposal that I have to refuse. Charles told me all his inner thoughts, his hopes, his ambitions all the things one doesn't usually talk about – he said it was my due. He was so terribly nice about it all and I did so loathe and despise myself for hurting him and disappointing him. He had such an idealistic vision of me – not a bit as I am now – but a sort of me without my larger faults.

One thing about this is that it has given me a sort of added self respect. I know all my faults and often I get horribly depressed, but from now on in my depressed bits I can always cheer myself up and brace myself by thinking that – awful though I may be – someone liked me well enough to want to live with me for the rest of his life.

Although she was clear enough in her own mind that she was not yet ready to settle down to married life, the proposal was important enough to make Isobel focus her mind on the problems that would confront her sooner or later, if she were to combine her career with being a wife and mother. Without any hint of resentment or even an awareness of how unfair it all was, she reflected on the attitude of a society which still saw the inequality between men and women as the natural order of things:

With a man – career is always first – wife and lover always second. Women on the other hand are fundamentally different. With them husband, lover and children all come first – career takes a second place – that is, in most women.

Women take much more arousing than men, once aroused however their emotions are much deeper and all-enveloping. Women are not properly aroused emotionally until after marriage – they do not indulge in the exchange of passionate felicity as do men, but once they have been sort of awakened up, emotions bubble up and obscure clear thinking.

36

After all, for countless centuries women's job has been to look after home, husband and children, and the thing is fundamental in us. Heaven knows, I am the world's most undomesticated creature, but if I married I should count it a whole-time job being a wife. Besides I think husbands no matter how sweet and understanding they may be about one's career, have always that inherent sense buried deeply in them, that being a wife is a whole time affair and he hates sharing you with anything even your job.

This my dear is probably quite wrong but it's just a pouring out of what I think, and what is in my mind.

Not all Isobel's letters are about her own thoughts and fears. She was always swapping information about mutual friends, offering advice and encouragement to Molly (who had become head girl at the Mount and was hoping to go on to read medicine at Girton College, Cambridge), and writing about what was going on around her:

I, my dear, am proceeding this après-midi, at the hour of three, to walk round the 10 miles or so which compose the Queen Mary! It was a great surprise when Hilary Rennie rang up and asked if I would like to see over her but I managed to stagger out my thanks. Why me? Of course I'm thrilled and it's terribly kind of them. I really feel that in honour of this momentous occasion, I'd better get a hair-wave and a face rejuvenation.

The Queen Mary was then the greatest liner ever built on Clydeside and its completion had done much to raise the morale of Scotland. Crowds queued just to get a glimpse of the ship in the yards and only the select few were allowed on board before the launching. But the great issue of the day was the abdication crisis and like almost everyone else in the country, the eighteen-year-old Isobel had her own views:

My opinions of the Mrs Simpson and King affair are a bit mixed. Divorce is not recognized by the English Church and the King as head of that church cannot marry a divorced woman. He, of course, realised that, and I think he has let himself and the country down badly by seeing this woman, and encouraging the friendship to the point he did. The fact that he suggested a Morganatic marriage [whereby Mrs Simpson would not have taken his rank or titles and any children from the marriage would not have been in line of succession] showed that he fully realized she could never be Queen. How any man at a time like the present could expose his country to a risk as the King did I don't know. If we had not had any born leader in the country things might have been a lot worse. Also, he had been trained for a 'Job' of his own. Many people nowadays cannot marry, because of lack of money or something else, so that the King was really no worse off than these people.

Of course, another bit of me thinks rather after the same fashion as you do only I do not think that any woman on earth is worth the sacrifice which the King made, and I only hope that she does her very best to make him very happy, as he must obviously love her very much.

During her third year, Isobel's studies took on a more practical nature and she found herself very much in the real world of over-crowded hospitals and patients suffering as much from the social evils of the day as from anything else. She learned more about the awfulness of life in working-class Glasgow and she told Molly: 'Personally I feel 80 with all the cares of the hospital upon my inadequate shoulders.' She learned that the damp and dirt led to wretched illnesses like pleurisy and diphtheria, pneumonia and tuberculosis, and that the illness led to even more wretched social problems. If it was the man who was in hospital, the wife and children had to go hungry because of the loss of wages; if it was the woman, the chances were that the children were left on their own all day while the man was at work and then most of the night while he was off drinking somewhere. She learned that 'home' didn't mean a lovely big house with servants to do the cooking and cleaning, but was more likely to be a two-roomed flat in a crumbling tenement block, where the parents shared one narrow, hole-in-the-wall bed and the rest of the family – whatever the number or age or sex – shared the other. They were likely to share the landing lavatory with six or more other families and had the pleasure of enjoying everyone else's cooking smells and domestic noises. Not only did such places breed disease, they bred violence, and back at the hospital, Isobel witnessed some of the consequences. Once a week, she spent a twenty-four-hour shift in the casualty department, supposedly studying the cases but in fact helping as frantic doctors and nurses fought to staunch the flow of blood from wounds caused by accident and by deliberate attack. In the daytime, it was usually the accidentally-injured who were brought in – shipyard workers suffering terrible burns from red-hot rivets falling on them; factory hands with slivers of metal nearly blinding them; children bleeding from a fall from a tenement window. At night came the victims of Glasgow's dangerous streets – the woman whose drunken husband kicked her in the face for no good reason; the fish-and-chip shop owner whose face was slashed when he would not give free chips to two young thugs; the gang-member who had been systematically beaten with bottles and bicycle-chains by another mob. Such happenings, such problems were so totally removed from anything young Isobel could have experienced in her own, genteel world that she would not have believed them if she had not seen them with her own eyes. But she did, and it meant that nothing was ever to shock her again. The pace of her growing up was quickening.

Sadly aware that she was losing touch with many of her school friends and almost by way of relief from her casualty experiences, Isobel started to take more of an interest in the general life of the university and was no longer so quick to turn down invitations. She joined the swimming club and proved to be so good at diving that she was awarded a blue. With her usual commitment, she trained regularly and took part in matches all over Britain and Ireland and, on one occasion, in the South of France. This was in the summer of 1938 and there was great nervousness about the intentions of Hitler and the Nazis. Austria had already been annexed and the British navy was at war-readiness. As Neville Chamberlain prepared for last-ditch talks with Hitler and Mussolini in Munich, it was decided that all British subjects should leave Europe and return home as quickly as possible. Isobel and her team-mates had their trip cut short and they joined the scramble to find seats on a train from Nice to the Channel ports. In their youthful disbelief that the world could be plunged into a second war, the girls converted the crisis into an adventure and overcame their discomfort by having a party with some of the French travellers. When they got back to Glasgow, their optimism about the war-threats proved – at least temporarily – to be justified. Mr Chamberlain proclaimed 'peace in our time' and the girls felt cheated at having their visit curtailed for no very good reason.

As she progressed through medical school, Isobel was discovering a new status. In the university, the younger students were very respectful and at home the girl servants were asking for medical advice. She enjoyed these new relationships and began to feel more confident that she had made the right decision about her career:

I am very lucky in having one of those single track minds. I have not very much imagination – or perhaps I have too much, but ever since I was quite small I have overcome all the opposition that was put in my path to prevent my becoming a doctor.

*

When she moved on to study obstetrics, any last vestige of doubt disappeared. Just after her twenty-first birthday, in June 1939, she delivered her first baby or, rather, first babies – twins. Isobel was thrilled and when the mother asked if she could call one of the little girls after her, she felt destined to a lifetime of delivering little Isobels. This was in Dublin, then regarded as one of the best centres for obstetrics in Europe, where she and several other Glasgow students had gone for a month's special study and practice. Again there was much more than medical experience to be gained. The squalor and poverty Isobel had learned about in Glasgow she saw at first hand in Dublin. Deceived initially by the city's Georgian facade, she quickly saw what lay behind much of the regal architecture – draughty, impractical homes where huge families huddled together as protection from both the cold and the economic threats of an apparently uncaring society. As she rushed around with her little black bag, packed with its midwifery needs, she often found there was not even room for her to sit down as she prepared to deliver the family's thirteenth or fourteenth child. She was constantly horrified by the sheer filth of the houses and worried incessantly about the total lack of hygiene which, of course, was a watchword of her hospital training.

But her Irish sojourn was not all work among the poor of Dublin. She also found time to join in the social whirl of cocktails, theatre-visits, supper parties, hunting and the famous horse show. As she adapted and unwound to the gentler tempo of Ireland, Isobel was able to forget the Nazi threat to world peace, but only temporarily. At the end of her midwifery session, she went for a short break to a friend's home in England, but for the second year running her summer plans were interrupted and she made yet another hurried retreat to Glasgow. There, on a warm, sunny Sunday morning, she learned that this was not another false alarm and she and her mother listened in dismay as Neville Chamberlain solemnly told the wireless audience that Britain was, once more, at war with Germany.

Isobel sought refuge in writing to Molly:

Well it's a very sad world n'est ce pas, and we are sadder and wiser women worse luck. The whole business makes my blood – in the language of Mr Chamberlain – boil. As however the boiling of my blood made no appreciable effect on the international situation, it has now gone off the boil like any neglected kettle.

Having calmed down, her next reaction was to join in the war effort:

Full of bright ideas for helping my fellow men, I got into the Royal Infirmary as casualty surgeon replacing an RNVR man. After two days of soul shattering activity we cleared the hospital out thus leaving ourselves with empty beds to cheer us. We now had nothing to do, and so we sat on empty beds, and surrounded by empty beds, in stygian darkness due to the combined effect of sandbags and black paper, while the balloon barrage waved happily overhead, keeping up our morale on gramophone records and news bulletins as supplied by the BBC. Oh it was all grand fun I don't fink. We waited all July for babies and now we wait for Hitler's little song birds to drop nest eggs upon our defenceless(?) civilian population. Tra-la-Tra-la however.

While like most of her young friends, affecting to be blasé about the whole affair, Isobel did confess to being worried about her current boyfriend, who was serving in the Royal Navy. After a gap of several years, she had met up with him in Dublin:

It was perfectly marvellous to go over there and find him completely unchanged and to be able to fall completely in love with him, on the spot pretty well. I got myself *almost* engaged. We meant to make it official as soon as he could come over and meet my family but now, however, he is with his ship somewhere around the British Isles. It is perfectly horrible to think of it even though people say blithely that the Navy is the safest service. What the hell do they know about it anyhow? My poor 'almost-fiancé' is somewhere in the cold Atlantic or the equally-cold North Sea. News of him is like manna and equally scarce. It isn't really news at all because all officers' letters are censored by the captain. He tells me that the wardroom is cockroach-haunted, that the ship's goat [sic] had a cannabalistic feast on one of his white kid gloves and that whenever they let off a broadside, my photo gets put between his best silk pyjamas in order that its glass may retain its pristine freshness.

As her letters show, Isobel had an astonishing facility for distancing herself from the grimmer realities of life and one has the impression that whatever terrible things may have been happening around her, they never really touched her, partly because of her very privileged upbringing and partly because she had created her own protective barriers. The most effective of these was her ability to damp down her emotions before they reached the surface, closely followed by her self-mocking sense of humour, which she used to denigrate a number of anxieties and self-doubts.

But if life was going on more or less as normal for Isobel and

41

her fellow students, that in itself created problems because, in their youthful idealism, they wanted to play some part in the war and their opportunities to do so were fairly limited. Isobel reacted by throwing herself into what was left of the society circuit and trying to forget about war in a hectic programme of social activities. These were slowed down a bit, when, out riding during the Easter break, she fell and badly twisted her knee. She had to go into hospital for an operation and, for the first time, saw things from the other side of the bed. Her attitude towards the nursing staff had already improved as the initial and mutual antagonism had eased off. Now she was completely won over to total sympathy for them when she saw how much work they had to do and how selflessly they did it. She became a model patient and, for two weeks, her little private room off the main ward became a haven where the nurses could put their feet up for five minutes and where she could greedily consume all the hospital gossip. It proved an invaluable addition to her medical education.

When she was back on her feet, Isobel was quickly caught up once more in the social round and, despite the fact that her final exams were looming, she decided to steal a week off from study to go to Cambridge for the May Balls. May Week in Cambridge is, of course, in June and that was the week in 1940 when Hitler chose to raid France and Holland. The balls were cancelled and for the third time Isobel caught the train home because of German interference with her social order. It did, however, allow her more time for study and she was therefore reasonably well prepared for the three weeks of exams in September. All that now stood between her and a degree, was her own nervous tension.

No one was really in any doubt about Isobel's chances of success. She had been a brilliant student who had always paced herself exactly right to pass exams with ease. And yet, when the results were finally posted on the university board, she could not believe she had made it. She said later that the moment she had longed for during the previous five years came as a terrible anticlimax and she found herself wandering around muttering, 'I am a doctor, I am a doctor,' without really convincing herself. It did not help that she suddenly realized that now all the family and institutional protection had come to an end and she would soon have to face the real world on her own.

Swimming party, 1930. Isobel has an 'A' on her costume. Her parents are on the far right.

In Glasgow, with a cousin's baby.

The Mount School's hockey team, 1934–5. Isobel is seated, on the extreme right.

Isobel at seventeen.

Isobel (on the left) walking with
friends at the Mount School.

Seaside snap, 1936.

A perfect summer holiday between the wars: Goathland, 1936.
Isobel is sitting in the stream.

Glasgow University swimming team, 1938. Isobel is seated, far right.

Geoffrey and Isobel on their wedding day.

CHAPTER 6

*I*sobel was not exactly ready for the real world. If her new qualifications and the much-respected title – Dr Marshall – suggested that she was now a highly-responsible citizen able to take her place in an adult society, her self-awareness told a different story. The truth was that, at twenty-two, she was still trying hard to grow up and to come to terms with the jumble of emotions and insecurities that seemed to plague her.

She still clung to the memories of her idyllic days at the Mount. It was there she had felt at her most confident, and it was the easy relationships with her old school friends that still mattered most to her. When she went to visit one of them and found that things had changed for the worse, she became quite distressed, as was obvious when she wrote to Molly Spencer:

I have often wondered what on earth made us so friendly? She is so terribly practical and so self-sufficient and capable. I am none of these. I'm absolutely helpless when it comes to practical things. I'm always scared of doing things in public in case people laugh at me. That never worried her. Then when we shared a study, she treated me with the indulgent contempt one holds towards a rather helpless infant, so I got into the habit of letting her do the things I wasn't good at, rather than trying them myself. I think that was disastrous both for my brains and my character.

This outpouring of her feelings to someone safely distant from day-to-day life was another symptom of her insecurity. She had developed such an outwardly-blasé attitude that she found it very difficult to have anything like a deep conversation with anyone:

I think one can usually express oneself a lot better on paper – I know I can. A combination of the famous Scottish reticence and my rather unique temper makes me rather difficult to get to know really well. However, I can always pour out my thoughts to you on paper knowing

43

that you will not dub me an awful ass.

Isobel's temper had been fearsome and it caused problems everywhere. The trouble was that she could not stand what she regarded as stupidity and her intelligence was such that an awful lot of people fell below her toleration level. She was, however, sensible enough to realize that she could not go on upsetting people, and it was as part of her growing-up process that she made tremendous efforts to curb her tongue. It was when she finally became aware that her outbursts made her look 'an awful ass' to her contemporaries that she learned to control herself. Once she achieved that, the young lady that the world saw was a real charmer – stylish and attractive, still a bit too boisterous to be elegant, but becoming more self-assured all the time.

Although she had had her doubts along the way, Isobel had known from the outset of her training that she wanted to become a family doctor in general practice, but during her final year she had decided to use up the time she had in hand over her classmates – she was a full year younger than most of them – to gain some extra hospital experience. Although it probably was not necessary because of her demonstrable ability, a little bit of judicious family string-pulling had guaranteed her a post as houseman to one of her father's old friends. He had agreed that she could do six months as a house surgeon and then six months as a house physician. It was an excellent opportunity and Isobel was looking forward to the challenge, but she felt badly in need of a break, and delayed her start for a few weeks while she had a holiday with an old schoolfriend in England.

The house she stayed at was in Nottinghamshire, and her friend's mother was a very generous hostess who was always giving parties for the officers from a nearby army camp. On previous visits, Isobel had heard a lot about Captain Geoffrey Barnett, one of the favourites of the house, and this time she actually met him. He was quite a lot older than her – sixteen years – and his reputation as a charmer did not help to make the opening conversations between them all that relaxed, but she persevered, just as she had been taught at the Mount. The more they talked, the more she liked him. She saw in him a gentleness allied to a strength of character missing from so many of her younger friends.

She discovered that he had gone to Haileybury – a generation behind Clement Attlee, then leader of the Labour Party, and one of the school's most famous pupils. After university he had,

44

again like Mr Attlee, become a lawyer. But beyond that there was little similarity, especially in their political views. As a serving officer, he was reluctant to express party beliefs, but Isobel guessed, correctly, that he was a staunch Conservative. In fact, before the war he had served for several years as a prominent member of Leicester City Council and was being talked about as a future Tory MP.

It was a very pleasant encounter and Isobel was flattered when the handsome captain suggested that they might meet again. However, as she was going back to Scotland to work in the hospital, she thought little more about it and rather assumed he was simply being polite in his usual charming way. She, in fact, prided herself in being able to read romantic situations with some expertness, and just before the holiday had given Molly the benefit of her most-recently acquired wisdom:

English love emotions cannot be judged by a Scot, as it is on this point that the two show their different nationalities. The more a Scotsman is in love, the quieter and more reserved he becomes, in fact almost avoiding the object of his affection. It's very misleading. An Englishman, from my short observation, appears, however, to get more and more oblivious of those around and he becomes more talkative and appears brighter than usual and you can obviously guess who is the object d'amour.

Unaware that she had hopelessly misread Captain Barnett's interest and therefore not knowing the impact she had made on him, she returned to Glasgow to carry on with the business of being a doctor, at the Royal Hospital for Sick Children.

As a houseman, she was expected to live-in at the hospital, but Isobel, being that rare phenomenon, a lady houseman, caused some difficulty over accommodation. The doctors' quarters were very rigidly for men only and she had to sleep in the nurses' home which, in a vain attempt to keep the sexes apart, was on the other side of the hospital. This had the disadvantage of causing a minor hiatus whenever she was on call. Those were the days before the bleeper paging-systems, and the housemen were roused for emergencies by urgent messengers. With Isobel, the messenger was always setting off in the wrong direction and by the time she eventually did get the call, it was always twice as urgent. However, she enjoyed being a houseman despite the long hours:

It's been grand fun dashing around in a white coat with respectful nurses hovering to do my bidding. It's been awfully bad for my head however which has increased in girth by inches. When you are always being phoned for to deal with emergencies, to quiet parents or to administer dope, it's apt to give you an exaggerated idea of your own importance – a bad thing.

From the tone of her letters, it is quite clear that Isobel was in many ways still well insulated from much of what was going on in the world around her. The reality for Britain in that summer of 1940 was that the war was going very badly. Hitler's armies, having already occupied Denmark and Norway, were then sweeping through the Low Countries and into France. Churchill formed his National Government and British troops tried in vain to stop the progress of the jackboots. Queen Wilhelmina was forced to flee from Holland and her country capitulated. The Belgian government withdrew from Brussels to Ostend where King Leopold finally ordered his men to surrender. The British army was pushed all the way back from Flanders and Ypres and Lille to Dunkirk, where a fleet of navy and civilian vessels staged the most remarkable rescue operation of more than 300,000 soldiers. Hitler proclaimed a war of total annihilation against all his enemies; Mussolini joined the Axis; Paris fell and the Vichy government signed an armistice; even the Channel Islands were occupied.

That, however, was not quite how Isobel saw it. She was much more readily influenced by the heroic picture of war:

We're swarming with RN here of course. It was at Greenock that Gracie Fields entertained the Navy and it was there too that I saw the landing of the Canadians – a really marvellous sight. I've been down to the Tail of the Bank as often as possible to see the various ships lying at anchor and looking perfectly marvellous.

Just then, the war never seemed to come any closer to her and she was able to add:

Life here hasn't been so awful despite the war. I've seen some grand plays – Dear Octopus – The Women – The Corn is Green – Design for Living – Geneva – and now the Doylé Carte are coming. There are few dances, only Red Cross ones and a few small regimental affairs, but there are lots of small parties and pleasant evenings spent with people on leave. I'm riding, swimming and skating as much as possible and then of course I occasionally do a spot of work.

Isobel was, of course, being somewhat blasé about her commitment and dedication but, later in the same letter, a little more of the truth is revealed despite her nonchalant,

46

throwaway style:

The McKenzie Andersons had a dance a week ago but I couldn't go as diphtheria had broken out in my two wards and what with swabbing throats of kids and nurses and getting them off to fever hospitals, I was too busy and anyway it would have been rather a risk to go.

Diphtheria, although now little-known in Britain, was then a scourge-like disease which swept across the world during the war years. Tyneside had already had an epidemic in 1939 and Scotland was to become one of the worst-hit European countries two or three years later. It was a ragingly-infectious disease that caused fever, accompanied in the more severe cases by an awful nasal discharge and a most offensive smell. The atmosphere in fever wards was foul and care of diphtheria patients, especially children, must have been a harrowing experience, but Isobel took it in her stride.

For her, this was the fulfilment of everything she had striven for over the five years at medical school. She had had to overcome many obstacles to follow in her father's footsteps, but now she was making a positive contribution to society the struggle had been worthwhile. Her commitment was total. And yet, when Captain Barnett proposed, she did not need to think twice about accepting, even though, as can be seen from her letters, she was fully aware of the conflicts of interest between career and marriage that would then confront her. The rationale she offered her friends was that he was the one man who she felt would be able to cope with her wilder excesses and who would, perhaps, keep her under the control she found so difficult to exercise herself. But as she admitted to Molly, there were other reasons: 'Geoffrey is tall and dark and quite nice-looking – even without prejudice. I'm terribly happy, my dear, being very much in love with him. We have a tremendous amount in common . . . love of the theatre (his grandmother was Henry Irving's leading lady), books, history, music, country life, horses, dogs and hunting. He has a very large sense of humour so life will be mirthful.'

After their first meeting, the captain had been as good as his word and had gone all the way from London, where he had been re-posted, to Glasgow to see her on two separate occasions. Beyond that, their only contact had been on the telephone, and that only spasmodically because of the eccentricities of wartime communications. But for Isobel it was enough. She always found it easy to make up her mind. She knew that she was in love, and though it was only a couple of months after their first meeting, she accepted his proposal with very little hesitation. Under normal circumstances there would have been a lengthy, well regulated engagement which would have allowed both families to perfect their arrangements. In wartime, with all the uncertainty of what tomorrow would bring, a short engagement was not only acceptable but also thought to be sensible. The wedding was set for January 1941. Isobel explained the situation to a sympathetic boss who readily agreed to release her from her contract and, three days after Christmas – which she had spent on duty – she left the hospital for the last time. In her short time as a houseman she had proved to be one of the most popular doctors in the building and everyone wanted to say their own farewell. She ended the day being ceremoniously trundled round all the wards on a theatre trolley and in something of an alcoholic haze.

Leaving the hospital and its centrally-heated security might well have been a traumatic, unhappy experience for Isobel, but she never really had the chance to find out quite how she felt, because she was immediately plunged into the frenzied activity of last-minute arrangements. She had already decided against a formal, white wedding and was half-expecting the reception to be a make-do affair for just family and close friends. Her mother had other ideas. Whatever other trouble he might have been causing, Herr Hitler was certainly not going to interfere with her daughter's great day if Mrs Marshall had anything to do with it. She counter-attacked with military precision. The local hotelier, who initially refused to arrange the reception because all his function rooms had been closed for the duration, was outflanked. After surrendering, he personally supervised the decorations and floral display. The brains behind Britain's food-rationing policy were outwitted and she acquired all the ingredients for an enormous wedding-cake. And she sorely tested the Auld Alliance by stockpiling abundant supplies of genuine French champagne. Embroiled as she was in the offensive, Isobel had no time to sit and think.

The wedding itself, in the event a triumphant affair, took place despite a welter of minor disasters. One of the bridesmaids was delayed for more than four hours on her journey from the Midlands and arrived in Glasgow just after midnight on the wedding eve. The second girl, coming from the North Country was even more unlucky and did not stumble in until five o'clock in the morning. By then a blanket of fog had descended on the city and there were fears that Geoffrey's brother, the best man, would not be able to fly in. He switched to the train and made it with only an hour to spare. Just when everything seemed to have settled down and the limousine had arrived to take the bridal party to church, the boiler of the house burst and flooded the kitchen, leaving the frantic maids paddling in nearly a foot of water. The air-raid siren sounded and the short journey to the church had to be delayed until the all-clear was given.

In all the confusion, no one remembered to tell Geoffrey that Isobel had changed her mind about what to wear and when she finally reached the church and walked down the aisle looking radiant in her traditional, full-length, white bridal gown, he had some doubts as to whether this was indeed his bride. Similarly, no one remembered to tell Isobel that Geoffrey had changed his mind about the honeymoon. The army had curtailed his leave to a mere seventy-two hours and when they finally slipped away from all the guests for a single night in Edinburgh, she had the masses of luggage she would have needed for a fortnight.

With Geoffrey's liberty fast-running out, the next evening they dashed to Edinburgh's Waverley Station to catch the overnight sleeper for London. But before she could start her journey into a new life, Isobel had somehow to squeeze all her luggage into the tiny sleeping compartment. She later admitted that there were eighteen cases in all, and her success in still finding room to sleep owed as much to her organizing ability as it did to her charm with the railway porters who helped her. She was not to be so lucky at the other end. In a bombing raid on London that night, the Luftwaffe had scored a direct hit on King's Cross and the train was stopped somewhere out in the suburbs, at a station without porters or taxi rank. Unruffled, despite the early-morning cold, Isobel cheerfully helped pile the cases on to an old railway trolley and trundled it outside, where she and Geoffrey then sat huddled together while they waited two hours for a taxi to take them across the bomb-scarred city to another station to catch another train for the last leg of their expedition to Salisbury in Wiltshire.

If Isobel had used the time to take stock of herself, she would have been well-pleased with the result. At twenty-two, well brought up, well educated, already a respected – if still inexperienced – member of an honourable profession, she had now made a very good marriage and could look forward to a happy, comfortable life with her thirty-eight-year-old, equally well bred, financially-secure husband. The war, and all its awfulness, would have been seen as a temporary disruption that would soon come to an end now that Mr Churchill was in charge of things.

Isobel and Geoffrey set up their first home in a sort of genteel transit camp – a big, old house run by what can only be described as a slightly-distressed gentlewoman and shared by three other army couples from Geoffrey's nearby headquarters. It was not exactly in the style to which Isobel had become accustomed. She wrote to her friend Molly about it:

We have the most minute flat. A long narrow sitting room, curtained in the middle to make dining and sitting rooms, a large bedroom, a large bathroom-cum-dressing-room, a minute kitchen and a microscopical larder. We daren't quarrel because there isn't enough room to allow two people to be angry.

As the landlady, with help from two other elderly gentlewomen, coped with all the cooking and domestic work, there was nothing much for Isobel to do during the day while Geoffrey was at his army office – despite her resolution to excel at the wifely art of home-making. There was an ancient harmonium in the house, but when she tried to play it, everyone else complained because it was so out of tune. She bought a wireless and became an avid listener, and also a reluctant walker, passing the time away rather than enjoying the exercise. She was delighted, therefore, to find that there were some stables nearby and she could sometimes go riding for a change.

On one of her gallops, she had an accident which could have been a tragedy but which also underlined her overwhelming concern with keeping up appearances. The horse threw her and bolted, leaving her unconscious and with a nasty head wound. When she came to, she managed to find a country cottage and the man there took her, blood-stained and bewildered, back to the stables where she had left her car. Thinking she was all right, he allowed her to drive home, but before she did so, she wrote a note, saying that if she was found unconscious or in a dazed state, she should not be assumed to be drunk, but should be taken to hospital for examination. As usual, Isobel's sense of propriety overrode all other considerations.

In fact, she drove home safely, collapsed on to her bed and lay there until Geoffrey returned. He took one look at her and rushed her off to the local doctor to have the wound stitched and dressed. The GP, unaware of Isobel's own medical knowledge and not realizing that she was able to hear him, explained to her worried husband that the injury looked bad enough to have possible serious consequences if she did not have complete rest for at least a month. Isobel did not argue with the doctor because she thought Geoffrey would be easier to handle. She waited until they were home and on their own and then started to play down the whole incident. She had forgotten that her lovely, new husband's gentle charm concealed a resolute firmness. He listened quietly to her ramblings, and then insisted she stayed in bed for every single day of the prescribed month.

At the end of it, she went home to Glasgow for a few days, but on her return to Wiltshire, she decided to make up for the enforced inactivity that had followed her accident by finding a job and somewhere more comfortable to live. The war made the first slightly easier for her as a woman, and the second much more difficult.

Ironically, under the circumstances, she accepted an offer of work that did not really suit her and which, from her letters to Molly Spencer, she did not seem to enjoy. Writing from the Greville Laboratory of Salisbury General Infirmary, she said:

As you can gather from this, I've gotten myself a job as assistant assistant pathologist in this laboratory. I hated it at first as I found the bugs lacked personality after the patients, but now I'm getting around and doing quite a lot of private work. My minor surgery for today being to extract a big bead from a baby's nose! We visit hospitals in Marlborough, Swindon, Shaftesbury, Winchester, the Isle of Wight etc. so I see the countryside. What amuses me is that my working hours are 10–5 and they pay me £250 per year, whereas as a house surgeon I worked like a slave and only got £50 per year.

Accommodation proved more easy to find, as Isobel met a lovely old couple who were willing to rent part of their big house. She would have preferred somewhere all to herself but the accommodation offered was better than their current home and she therefore settled happily for sharing with the owners. It was hardly an ideal property, however. The kitchen was actually a lean-to greenhouse, complete with a gnarled old vine that grew in through a gap in the glass, up behind the ancient gas stove and over the sink. The occasional grapes that appeared were very small and very sour. In addition, the toilets seldom flushed and water could never be heated to more than tepid, but Isobel loved it all, and, as she got on so well with the elderly landlords, she was happy.

It was now that she discovered a king-size gap in her expensive education. She knew absolutely nothing about looking after a home and a husband all by herself. It is true to say that her mother had once arranged a cookery course, on the assumption that her daughter would one day have to be practical, but the lessons turned out to be for advanced ladies already at the *cordon bleu* stage, and while Isobel learnt how to concoct soufflés and suchlike, the rudiments of preparing an ordinary, meat-and-two-veg dish were well beyond her. The problem was further aggravated by her total ignorance of the finer points of shopping for essentials. All her expeditions had been to the more stylish fashion salons of Glasgow, and she had never actually gone into a greengrocery or butcher's shop before. The result was that her initial forays in search of provisions caused her acute embarrassment. She had no idea about weights or volumes and asked for 'some' carrots, or, when pressed for more accurate guidance, suggested 'about a stone or two'. She was saved from constant over-buying only by the friendly advice of the local shop-keepers and the wartime rationing of food. But perseverance had long been an important part of young Isobel's make-up and she quickly had the whole business taped. With the help of several recipe books, she soon learnt how to exploit the lean-to kitchen's primitive facilities and became an excellent cook.

While mastering the art of domestic self-defence, she found that the only way to stop the constantly advancing dust and dirt was to bring in more troops. She employed a 'daily' in time to stop any real roughening of her hands and she was more than happy to acquiesce when the good lady gradually took over the wide range of domestic duties and ended up virtually running the Barnett household. In those days, such a woman was popularly known by the middle and upper classes as 'a treasure' and certainly this one proved to be exactly that to the young and inexperienced Isobel, who was now enjoying married life:

Molly, don't ever even think of doing what I once thought of doing i.e. remaining single to pursue a career! I know I've never been so utterly happy and unrestless in my life before. Having been a rather lonely child I appreciate tremendously the companionship of marriage, having someone to share your interests, listen to your views, give you advice and ask your advice. I used to hate the lonely feeling of setting off for parties and dances alone, and longed for some moral support. I love entertaining Geoffrey's friends. Our entertaining is of the most casual variety, but people seem to like it, and that makes me feel I'm really doing something for Geoffrey.

In her contentment and without the distraction of the chores, she was able to concentrate her mind on trying to find a more interesting occupation than the dull routine of the pathology laboratory, and once again luck was on her side. One of the younger doctors at the local surgery was called up for army service and she was invited to replace him as a locum. It was the chance she had begun to think might never come her way. All her father's warnings about the attitude towards women doctors had already proved to be justified (which partly explains her readiness to accept the unsuitable laboratory job in the first place) and even her smart-set contacts had so far failed to come up with any partnership offers. But now, with so many men going to the front, hard-line male-chauvinism was being eroded by the acknowledgment that women had major contributions to make, which were acceptable in the cause of the war effort. Isobel took full advantage of the situation and threw herself energetically and enthusiastically into the work for which she had so long trained and dedicated herself – looking after the sick. The sick were not quite so enthusiastic about their new family doctor. The patients in that Salisbury practice were no less conservative than the medical establishment. They did not particularly like change of any description and when they suddenly found a young slip of a girl coming round with her doctor's little black bag, it was much too radical for comfort. One stern-faced lady would not even let her into the house, closing the door on her with a very firm and frosty 'Not today, thank you.'

Again however, the force of prevailing circumstances militated in Isobel's favour. If the patients did not succumb to her youthful ministrations, they stayed sick. There were not enough male doctors to go round. Slowly but surely she won acknowledgement as a real doctor and, with her easy charm, built up a rapport with most of them.

Trying to be a good GP was very hard work. It meant a very early start in the morning for the nine o'clock surgery, going without lunch most days, and seldom finishing the round of house-calls before seven o'clock in the evening. Isobel, however, enjoyed every moment of it, and at last began to feel she was making a worthwhile contribution to society. And society paid her back – in the shape of provisions that were almost unobtainable under strict rationing. Most shops then served

53

only regular customers and kept certain items under the counter for special customers. To her grateful patients, the young doctor had become quite special and their collective generosity helped to mitigate the excesses of food shortages by ensuring that the Barnett larder was always reasonably well-stocked.

There was one minor threat to Isobel's pleasant existence. But it was only from the army and, against the combined guile and charm of the captain's wife, the colonels never had a chance. The first hint of disruption came one evening when Geoffrey returned home and said he was going to be posted to another depot at Bulford. It was too far from Salisbury, especially because of the petrol rationing, for him to travel each day and the implication was that they would have to move. If Isobel was dismayed by the news, she did not show it, but neither did she simply accept it. Next day, she took a break from work and drove over to Bulford for a careful reconnaissance of the area. She was not very impressed with what she saw and decided that it would really be much more sensible to stay put in Salisbury. All she had to do was convince Geoffrey and the army that his transfer was not a good idea. As a first step in her campaign of gentle persuasion, she invited the colonel and his wife to dinner, and then she took a page out of her mother's war book. Following Mrs Marshall's example of the wedding feast, she begged and borrowed an astonishing array of food and drink, creating an absolutely slap-up meal and making a nonsense of the rationing system. There was a delicious soufflé to start, followed by a nice fat chicken, accompanied by a bottle of claret. This was followed by liqueurs, real coffee and even Turkish cigarettes. Always a gracious hostess, Isobel piled on a double helping of charm when the colonel and his lady arrived for this veritable banquet. Not once did she mention the possibility of Geoffrey being posted, and neither did the colonel, then or later. The Barnetts stayed in Salisbury for the rest of the war, and Isobel – quietly schooled by Geoffrey to accept a more gracious pace of living – became the district's most-popular hostess.

Almost regardless of the war, Isobel and Geoffrey lived the high life whenever possible and spent many of their leaves in London, staying with friends and enjoying what was left of the capital's night-life. When they returned from one trip in the spring of 1943, Isobel became quite ill and, after a prompt self-diagnosis, asserted that the oysters she had eaten in London must have been off, because she was suffering from food-poisoning. Two weeks later, a more experienced colleague convinced her that she had misread the symptoms. She was pregnant. She and Geoffrey were overjoyed, and they were both relieved to find that their elderly landlords were equally thrilled at the prospect of becoming unofficial grandparents.

Trouble developed, however, when the local nursing-home could not accept the booking for Isobel's confinement. They were already fully-booked and there was nothing she could do or say that would make any difference. The baby was due around Christmas, so towards the end of November, Isobel caught the train back to Glasgow, leaving the anxious Geoffrey at the end of the unreliable telephone line. At home, Isobel wallowed in the unaccustomed luxury of her mother's all-embracing attention and patiently waited for the signs that the baby's arrival would be soon – and waited, and waited. Christmas came and went, as did New Year's Eve. Tension mounted and Geoffrey spent hours on the telephone, whenever the Post Office permitted. Two weeks later than expected: 'To Geoffrey and Isobel Barnett (née Marshall), a son, Alastair, on 4 January, 1944.'

CHAPTER 7

To most of her friends' surprise and not a little disapproval, Isobel decided she wanted to get back to her job as a locum as soon as possible, and although the more conventional Geoffrey was not quite so keen on the idea, he for once gave way, and it was agreed that a full-time, living-in nanny would have to be found. The search was not easy, but after numerous interviews and the careful checking of references, they finally hired a woman straight out of the top drawer of British nannies. For years she had been raising the top people's children while they had attended to the great affairs of state or to the good management of industry, and among her former charges were several little lordships, two or three honourables and the daughter of a Conservative MP. It was a formidable record and from the moment she arrived she made it perfectly clear that she would brook no interference in her methods of child-care and child-development. Uncertain as to how to cope with such assertiveness in other people, Isobel happily gave way and allowed her *carte blanche* in Alastair's care and control. Nanny's influence was considerable and when she knew she had a firm grip on the Barnett household, she declared that the old house, with its lack of modern amenities and its ageing landlords, was no place to bring up a child. It says much for her training in the stately homes of England that Geoffrey and Isobel meekly acknowledged her authority and immediately began the task of looking for other, more suitable accommodation, eventually settling on an inconveniently-sited but spacious house which suited nanny's requirements.

Isobel was not at all maternalistic – referring to the new baby as 'the soggy bundle' – and at first she was quite happy to delegate her day-to-day responsibilities to nanny. It was nice not to be burdened by the essential routines and lovely to come home each day to a contented, well fed, sweet-smelling baby. She was still enjoying being a family doctor and she knew she was getting the best of all worlds – but then why shouldn't she? It was what she had always aimed for and there was no reason why she should not exploit her success. But as Alastair emerged from babyhood and entered the more interesting stages of his development, she found it more of a wrench to leave him in the mornings and could hardly wait to get back to him in the evenings. She worried more about all his childish illnesses and found it increasingly difficult to leave it all to nanny.

When, on one occasion, he was clearly suffering from something more serious than one of the usual childhood complaints like mumps or measles and it was eventually diagnosed as meningitis, an alarmed Isobel found it very difficult to cope while still doing her doctor's rounds. She decided to give up her job in the general practice to stay at home and look after him herself. From her experience in the Glasgow children's hospital, she knew only too well how serious meningitis could be. She knew that it carried the likelihood of brain damage and that only a few years earlier half the cases had proved fatal. Luckily, however, Alastair's condition turned out to be less serious than was first thought. He was suffering from the aseptic variety of meningitis, which in fact was quite common in children and was little more than a mild virus infection. But although he was soon back on his feet, the fright seems to have scared his mother somewhat, and from then on, even after he had grown-up, she kept a doubly-cautious eye on him. However, she did her best to conceal her fear and never talked about it to anyone other than her husband. For example, it never featured in any of the continuing correspondence with her confidante, Molly Spencer. Indeed, as time went by, her letters became less and less informative as she lost her girlish enthusiasm for writing, and with it much of her style: 'My dear Molly, I thought I had better drop you a line about August. I enclose the route which we use ... Excuse hurried scrawl, all my love, Isobel.'

Isobel's fears, together with any thoughts she might have had about going straight back to work once Alastair was well again, were very quickly set aside when Geoffrey was released from the army, as it now accepted that the end of the war was clearly in sight. In the four years since their marriage, the Barnetts had never really been able to feel settled, because of the uncertainty of the war, but now they had the prospect of putting down roots. It was a heady feeling and, as they had always intended,

Geoffrey went back to Leicestershire to find a house. But this was easier said than done. As Geoffrey scoured the villages around Leicester for month after month, Isobel began to feel almost abandoned in Salisbury, and finally it was decided that she and Alastair should join Geoffrey at his mother's house. It was far from satisfactory because his brother had just returned from a POW camp in Germany and there were still two army officers billeted there, making the place very overcrowded. But it was much better than continued separation and, as the day Isobel chose to travel to Leicestershire turned out to be VE Day – 8 May, 1945 – her reunion with Geoffrey was celebrated against the background of bells pealing out all across Britain.

The frustrating search for a house continued, spurred on by the overcrowding at the Barnett family residence and the inevitable strain of living with in-laws. They assiduously followed up every single lead in the forlorn hope that it might take them down a garden path to something habitable, but it was a frustrating business and Isobel's natural good humour was stretched dangerously thin before they were finally shown round a cottage that actually lived up to the estate agent's boasts. Although it was small, it was very pretty and it looked as if it would suit their needs, at least in the short-term. They were both very relieved when their offer was accepted and Geoffrey used his professional advantages to press on very quickly with the legalities. But while the details were being finalized, he took his mother to look round and she liked what she saw so much that she surprised him with the suggestion that she move into the cottage and they stay on in the big house. Although it seemed a very generous offer, Isobel was not terribly keen on the idea. She had fallen in love with her cottage and was not particularly enamoured of staying in the big, draughty house. But Geoffrey saw the logic of the suggestion. His mother was in her seventies, the house was becoming something of a liability to her and the cottage was really much smaller than they had wanted. With his customary firmness, he talked his wife round and she reluctantly agreed to the swap.

Despite her initial reluctance, acquiring the house was very important to Isobel: it meant that she could start to put down roots. From her wedding four and a half years earlier – when she had packed her past in those eighteen suitcases – she had led a gypsy-like existence. Until now, the uncertainty of war had precluded any semblence of an ordered life. It was like starting over again, and it was not easy for her to settle down in

Leicestershire. She only knew her husband's family and one or two other people she had met on previous holiday visits. Nor did she have a job that would take her into contact with the local residents. Even the domestic staff she managed to hire were foreigners – Hungarians – who could speak only a few words of English and who quarrelled noisily with Slavonic passion.

Geoffrey, on the other hand, was able to slide comfortably into his old life-style. He had moved back six months before Isobel, had re-joined his solicitor's partnership and was once again embroiled in local politics. He had resumed his seat on Leicester City Council and had just been elected an alderman. With local government in some confusion in the aftermath of the war, it was hard work trying to pick up the pieces and for aldermen like Geoffrey, it meant long, tedious hours at council and committee meetings.

All this added to Isobel's difficulties because she was left on her own most evenings in the week, with little to do but read, listen to the radio or play the piano. It was not an especially happy time for the gregarious young doctor but instead of letting it get her down, she responded by going into politics herself.

She did not aspire to the weighty responsibilities of the city council, but agreed to stand for election to the rural district council – and, of course, won. It had all begun as a joke as far as Isobel was concerned. One of the local Conservatives had asked her if she might be interested in joining the council and she had responded by laughing it off as a silly idea. But when she told Geoffrey about it, he could not understand why she thought it funny, and insisted in his civic-minded way that she consider it seriously. She knew nothing about local government and her impression was that it was all rather stuffy and uninteresting, but eventually, as much in deference to her husband as anything else, she agreed to put her name forward as a Conservative candidate. The election was rather a genteel affair, with Isobel expected simply to visit as many of the villagers as possible and charm them into voting for her instead of the Labour man. There were no meetings or platform speeches and, unlike the big-city hustings, there was no exchange of insults between the candidates. Isobel found it all great fun and enjoyed meeting people. She was surprised when she won and in fact became quite upset on behalf of the defeated candidates. Although she was a winner by temperament, she would have preferred it if there did not have to be losers.

She was also surprised when she went to the first meeting of the council and found that the level of debate was far from the parish pump. Instead, the discussions were about the post-war problems of overcrowding and bad housing conditions. It was nothing like the Glasgow she had learned something of while doing her medical training, but in a way it had more impact on her. Perhaps because they were less awful, she could identify more with the deficiencies of Leicestershire, and now that she was a councillor, she actually had some responsibility to try to do something about them. It was a tremendous challenge, and Isobel was never happier than when she was squaring up to a problem.

Despite using up a lot of her energy on council business, Isobel also found time to take on more locum work and soon became very popular with GPs all around Leicester as she stood in for them while they had a holiday – quite often the first they had been able to have since before the war. At home she had a firm grip on domestic matters too. Young Alastair had outgrown nursery and nanny and was now settled in the routine of daily attendance at the local kindergarten, regular visits to other children's parties and weekly lessons from a dance teacher. The two Hungarians had been tamed – at least to the degree where they fought less noisily – and they looked after all the household chores in a gently eccentric manner.

For Isobel, it was a busy and exciting life and she enjoyed every moment of it, easily putting behind her the loneliness and dullness of her first few months in Leicestershire. It was Aneurin Bevan who checked her pace, at least temporarily. He was, of course, the architect of the new National Health Service which was launched in 1948, and his scheme did not allow GPs to work only part-time. Isobel, galled that an arch-Socialist should interfere with her freedom, had to opt to go into full-time practice or give up altogether. With Alastair to think about, she decided, at the ripe old age of 30, that she would have to retire. It was quite a wrench, but she always had at the back of her mind that she would take medicine up again when Alastair went off to boarding school, and that somehow made it easier for her to accept. In the meantime, she turned her attention from the sick to the criminal, allowing her name to go forward for selection as a magistrate. As this new job started to take up some of the slack in her timetable, the young councillor Dr Isobel Barnett, JP became irrevocably locked into public life, and from then on almost everything she did was destined to attract attention, some of it not entirely welcome.

Not long afterwards, the Conservatives won control of the city council and Geoffrey became chairman of the vitally-important housing committee. Two years later, in 1951, he was elected leader of the Conservative group and the most powerful man on the council. Isobel, operating on the lower political plain, became the first woman chairman of the Barrow-upon-Soar Rural District Council. Then within twelve months, Geoffrey was invited to be Lord Mayor of Leicester. If he accepted, it would mean that for a year, neither he nor Isobel would be able to call their life their own. Isobel, as always, was positive. It was a great honour and a fitting tribute to his years of commitment, of course he must accept. The decision was made much easier by the fact that Alastair was now eight and would be going off to boarding school just before the inauguration. The heavy list of civic engagements would not, therefore, affect him. Geoffrey accepted the invitation with some nervousness.

On 20 May, 1952, in a ceremony of splendid pomp, Geoffrey and Isobel were duly installed as Lord Mayor and Lady Mayoress of Leicester. It was a wonderful moment for them both, with Geoffrey, handsome and dignified in his mayoral robes and Isobel looking absolutely regal in her long, silk-brocade dress and a diamond tiara. She was the city's youngest Lady Mayoress and certainly one of the most beautiful.

She took to her new role instantly. She loved all the pageantry that surrounds any Lord Mayor and was delighted to be the centre of attention wherever she went. Her days were all mapped out for her and there was the mayoral Daimler to take her to the endless series of meetings, fêtes, bazaars, lunches, dinners and presentations. Almost every organization in the city demanded at least one civic visit during the year, and Isobel, already adept at small talk – the importance of which had been drummed into her at her boarding school – became expert at making other people feel relaxed and comfortable.

Suddenly three weeks into the civic year, Geoffrey collapsed and was rushed to hospital. It was appendicitis and, despite his protests that it would disrupt his diary of daily engagements, he had an emergency operation that put him out of action for several weeks. Isobel, who until then had played more of a decorative than practical role, suddenly found she had to take on some of the more important duties. Her first solo venture was to host a dinner for a group of German local government officials. When they arrived for pre-dinner drinks, she was careful to make sure that each guest was specifically looked after by other members of the council, and finally turned her attentions on the man who had led the group into the Lord Mayor's Parlour. In the traditional manner of addressing foreigners, she spoke very slowly and loudly and was very pleased when it was obvious that she was making herself understood. However, her self-congratulations were soon stifled when the Town Clerk, coming across to join the conversation, remarked: 'Ah, I see you've already introduced yourself to our new Deputy Town Clerk!'

Isobel was quite relieved, in more ways than one, when Geoffrey recovered from his operation and was able to carry out the duties once more.

In the summer, the diary was carefully manipulated so that they could have at least a short break from the treadmill. They collected Alastair from boarding school and went off to their favourite seaside resort, Tenby, on the south Pembrokeshire coast. As usual, they stayed at the Atlantic Hotel, right on the seafront, overlooking the magnificent South Beach. Isobel was still an enthusiastic swimmer and Alastair, at the learning stage, enjoyed practising his dog-paddle, despite the chilly water. But a couple of days after they arrived, Alastair got caught in a current that was too strong for his inexpert strokes and began to drift away from the shore, while his parents sunbathed on the sand. Geoffrey, observing this and thinking he was venturing out a bit too far, swam out to bring him in. However, he too got caught in the current and, still weak after his operation, was unable to make any headway against the ebbing tide. Once she realized the danger, Isobel immediately plunged into the water and with all her experience was very quickly alongside them both. By this time Alastair was very frightened and was clinging so tightly to his father that they were both in danger of drowning. All Isobel could do was tread water and keep the three of them afloat. Even she could not overcome the current and they drifted further and further out to sea. At last someone saw they were in serious difficulties and raised the alarm, putting out a call for the lifeboat crew. While there was a frenzy of activity on the shore, Isobel suddenly realized that they had come diagonally across the bay and the current was now moving inshore, so with the little energy she had left she started to swim again with Geoffrey and Alastair in tow. After what must have seemed an eternity, they were being helped on to the beach. They had been in the water for more than three-quarters of an hour and Geoffrey was totally exhausted, but still his sense of responsibility was uppermost. As he was being given first aid, he asked the attendant policeman to ring the town's mayor and explain that he would not be able to keep the appointment that had been made for him to pay his respects. Young Alastair showed the same *sang-froid* by expressing anxiety about being late for a children's party back at the hotel. Indeed, the incident would probably have been very quickly forgotten if the local journalist had not heard about it, and knowing who the near-victims were, sent a graphic story to the Leicestershire newspapers. It made the headlines, of course, but one of the billboard writers went too far with: 'Lord Mayor's Drowning Accident', and caused great anxiety to many of their friends and relatives.

Later that same summer, in the middle of August, there were terrible thunderstorms all around the south west and East Anglian coastlines, causing disastrous flooding in both areas. In Leicester, Geoffrey immediately set up a Lord Mayor's appeal fund and he and Isobel added to their already heavy workload by undertaking a series of money-raising ventures. The response was amazing. On the first day, the money started to pour in and Isobel sat by the phone logging offers of both practical and financial help – a lorry load of wellingtons; clothing; blankets; shoes; and the names of local people prepared to go to the disaster areas to help clear up the devastation. In the end, the Leicester appeal raised more than £56,000.

It was during this year as Lady Mayoress that Isobel honed to perfection her aptitude for always doing exactly the right thing at the right time. The civic path to success traverses a minefield of protocol, yet she picked her way through the danger zones with immense skill and delicacy. Of course, there were mistakes, but somehow her elegance or charm eased every difficult situation.

All her coolness was needed one day when she and Geoffrey turned out for a great parade of the city's uniformed youth organizations. The order of ceremony entailed an inspection of the 'troops' followed by a march-past, with the Lord Mayor taking the salute. At the head of quite a large official party, the Lord Mayor and Lady Mayoress proceeded in stately fashion to inspect the serried ranks, stopping every now and then to chat to some of the youngsters. When that was over, the civic dignitaries turned away and walked sedately towards the distant saluting base. But the young man in charge of the parade was so keyed up that he gave the marching orders too soon and with still more than a hundred yards to the dais, Isobel heard the crunch of a thousand and more boots rapidly catching up with the brass. Panic set in. The senior officer in the group broke into a gallop, he was followed by a noble lord and two other, older men who managed a kind of trot. Geoffrey, in his heavy chain of office, wisely resisted the temptation to run, but increased his pace to a very brisk rate that would have satisfied an infantry sergeant-major. The Lady Mayoress was determined that whatever happened, whether or not the marching boots caught up with her, she would not forfeit her dignity and poise. The biggest cheer of the day was reserved for her as, with outward calm, she stepped on to the platform only a couple of yards ahead of the parade.

There is no doubt that Isobel thoroughly enjoyed the mayoral year and was justifiably proud of the way she and Geoffrey had carried it off. Writing about civic heads some time later, she said: 'They are an essential part of English life and they provide the rallying figurehead for a city's loyalty and pride.' The Barnetts had proved how successful they were in that figurehead role by the response they won from the people of Leicester when they launched their appeal for the flood-disaster victims. 'Our year in chains,' said Isobel, 'was very, very special to both of us.'

The mayoral year began in May 1952, and special as it was for the city's handsome civic couple, the following year was to prove even more extraordinary. With only a few weeks in office left, Geoffrey received a letter from 10 Downing Street. It was signed by the Prime Minister, Winston Churchill, who said that in preparing a special Honours List to mark the Queen's Coronation, he was putting forward Geoffrey's name for a knighthood. This was in recognition of his service to local government and, in particular, his efforts in raising money for the flood victims. The thrill and elation in the Barnett household must have been very difficult to stifle, but stifle it they must until the official announcement was made on Coronation Day. The secrecy was very much easier for the more reserved Geoffrey than for his wife, whose normal exuberance was doubled by her pride in him. Luckily it was a particularly busy civic period, with Coronation preparations adding to the hectic duties of a Lord Mayor and Lady Mayoress, so that the time seemed to pass very quickly and Isobel was able to contain herself.

In the run-up period to the Coronation, Geoffrey won two tickets in his London club's ballot for seats over-looking the royal route to Westminster Abbey on Coronation Day, 2 June. Had he still been Lord Mayor – his term finished a fortnight earlier – he would, of course, have had tickets for the Abbey itself, but Isobel was nevertheless excited at the prospect of a ring-side seat for the magnificent procession through the streets of London. At the last moment, however, Geoffrey agreed to stand-in for the new Lord Mayor and stay in Leicester to carry out all the essential civic duties on the great day, such as crowning the local Coronation Queen. For once the temptation was too much for Isobel. Her better self was given a back seat and while her husband was making his first public appearances as *Sir* Geoffrey, she – now Lady Barnett – was sitting on a balcony in London watching the greatest of all Britain's ceremonial spectacles.

The date of Geoffrey's investiture was announced soon after and Isobel learned that she would be accompanying him to Buckingham Palace on Tues, 30 June, her thirty-fifth birthday. The perfection of the day at the Palace, with more tradition and ceremonial and an even better ring-side seat, was marred only by the absence of young Alastair, who had gone down with chicken-pox only the day before and was unable to make the trip to London.

Before the anti-climax of her royal month could set in, Isobel found herself in the throes of moving house. Although she had been quite happy in Geoffrey's family home, she had persuaded him that a new residence was a good idea and they had been looking half-heartedly at properties over the previous couple of years. Just before the Coronation she had spotted a house she liked, and only days after the investiture, contracts were exchanged and she was able to plan the move into the White House, a lovely Georgian house right in the main street of the tiny village of Cossington. It was to be her home for the rest of her life.

In the middle of the upheaval of moving house, Isobel had a letter from the BBC in Birmingham asking her to take part in 'Town Forum', a discussion programme newly-switched from radio to television. At that time – in the early 1950s – television was still trying to find its feet and had nowhere near the same prestige or pulling power as radio. Isobel was also embroiled in the last-minute preparations for the family's summer holiday in Pembrokeshire, and so her first reaction was to decline the invitation. As so often was the case, it was her husband who persuaded her to think again. He had no idea of what was to follow for Isobel and himself, but he did feel that there was tremendous potential in the newer medium and declared it would be silly not to give it a try. When he added that the packing could wait, she promptly agreed and accepted the invitation.

She knew something of what would be expected of her because she had already taken part in the radio version of the programme, when a BBC man happened to hear her making a speech of thanks as chairman of her housing committee. She therefore set off happily for Birmingham, where, in the improbable setting of the main fire station, she was the only woman on the panel of four speakers. Before an audience of firemen and their friends – which dramatically thinned out at one point when there was an emergency call – she and the other panellists exchanged views on a range of topical issues raised by the chairman – education, road safety and space travel.

If Isobel felt nervous on her first screen appearance, she hid it very well. Most women would have been quite disconcerted by the offstage technician who, when testing the microphone from a position where he could not see, mistook her for a man because of the timbre of her voice – rich and deep, but not at all masculine. She simply threw her head back and gave a long throaty laugh that enchanted everyone and left no one in any doubt about her femininity.

Although it was still a long way behind radio in terms of audience, there was a great novelty value in television – especially after its spectacular coverage of the Coronation – and the programme, not the sort that would rate more than a couple of lines in today's newspapers, was extensively reviewed. Not surprisingly, the columnists devoted most of their column inches to Isobel. It may be that they would in any case have been enthusiastic about this beautiful, young 'unknown', but with the added status of her being *Lady* Barnett, they went overboard. This gave the cue to the rest of Fleet Street and the next day the White House was almost like a studio, as Isobel was asked to pose for press photographs in dozens of different settings and positions. Geoffrey was not particularly impressed by the sudden attention. 'I didn't think you were all that good,' he grumbled.

There was some relief from the publicity the following day, when the Barnetts set off for the sandy beaches of Tenby again. But the press managed to find them there, and more photographic sessions followed, with Geoffrey keeping well in the background. Eventually the furore died down, and Isobel was able to relax and enjoy a well earned break. She was sitting on the cliffs one morning, looking out over the sea at nothing in particular, when she was asked to go back to the hotel to take a phone call from London. It was from a man called Maurice Winnick, who owned the rights of television's most popular panel game, 'What's My Line?' He had read about her in the newspaper, he said, and he wondered if they might meet to discuss the possibility of her appearing on the show. It was a call that was to stand her life on its head.

CHAPTER 8

*T*he success of many a venture lies in the essential simplicity of the idea behind it. Few television programmes can have been more successful than 'What's My Line?' and certainly none have been simpler in concept. It was as uncomplicated as a children's guessing game and gave just as much pleasure to millions of viewers throughout the 1950s and early 60s.

One of the early imports from American television, the idea was to invite people of different occupations to offer a minimal hint – the famous mime – to a panel of personalities who were then expected to guess the job. There were no prizes, only that smug feeling of self-satisfaction for the winners or the excitement of at least having tried for the losers.

The programme made its first inauspicious appearance on the embryonic BBC Television in the summer of 1951. The first contestants asked to sign in by Eamonn Andrews – then best-known as a boxing commentator – were a barrow-boy, a chauffeuse, a cocktail-shaker and a swimming instructress. It may have been because they presented little difficulty to the panel – Marghanita Laski, Barbara Kelly, Jerry Desmonde and Ted Kavanagh – that the show did not exactly take off. It seemed all very lack-lustre and no one at the BBC was particularly happy with the programme. The producer admitted that it was probably his fault for keeping too close to the original American format for the British audience. But in those pioneering days of the tiny, nine-inch, purplish screen, good ideas were not discarded lightly and over the next few weeks the producer tried various combinations of panellists and chairmen as well as several other experiments. It looked at first as if the chemistry just was not right and one particularly unsuccessful line-up featured Gilbert Harding as chairman. Gilbert was one of radio's most famous voices and although he was to become one of television's more improbable stars, he was then best-known for his gruff, acerbic manner. His singular lack of diplomacy lost him the job and it went back to Eamonn Andrews, Harding being invited instead to become a panellist. This time everything clicked, the audience responded with enthusiasm and the programme shot up the ratings to become one of the most popular of the week. Within three months, it was given the ultimate television accolade – the planners' permission to expand from a half-hour to forty-five minutes. By the time Lady Barnett received her call two years later, it was dominating the weekend viewing at peaktime on Sunday evenings and was very much part of the British way of life.

Not surprisingly, Isobel was hesitant about accepting an invitation to audition for the programme, because she did not see how she, an unknown housewife, could fit in with the famous personalities. There was also, at the back of her mind, the nagging fear that appearing on television might make her public property even more than she already was as Lady Barnett. In the end, she agreed to see Maurice Winnick in London for no other reason than she knew she would kick herself later if she did not go. At the interview, she saw a film of the American original – sponsored by a deodorant company whose commercial promised to 'make the armpit the charm pit' – and was told that the vacancy on the panel was for a woman who would be 'the knowledgeable ferreter-out ... the blood-hound who pursues each clue, however nebulous, to the bitter end,' and who was quiet and calm and logical and sophisticated. The ever-modest Isobel retreated to Leicestershire convinced that she would hear no more about the programme. Nor did she – until a few weeks later, when a Fleet Street newspaperman rang to ask for her reaction to being chosen to join the panel. That call was followed in quick succession by all the other national papers and Isobel was suddenly aware of the astonishing grip 'What's My Line?' had on viewers and its consequent value as a source of interest for journalists. But she did not quite believe it all until a day or two later when the formal letter from the BBC arrived, offering her five appearances on the show.

There was, of course, a great deal of curiosity about how this elegant but little-known lady from the genteel Shires would fit into the very different world of showbusiness. What, for example, would she be called on the show? 'I hope they'll call me Isobel,' she replied, forgetting for a moment her courtesy title. The next day's headline read: 'Lady Barnett says "Call me Isobel".' The following day she was a little shaken to read that

Gilbert Harding was unlikely to connive at such informality. Living up to his reputation as a cantankerous and pedantic stickler for the proprieties of social decorum, he told the press: 'I should not dream of addressing anyone whom I did not know well by their Christian name. I shall call her Lady Barnett.'

Gilbert was the most formidable and, in many ways, the most unlikely member of the panel. He had come to television via an astonishing career that had lurched from trainee Anglican priest to Roman Catholic lecturer at a Benedictine monastery in Canada; from newspaper correspondent in Cyprus to policeman in Bradford; from studying for the Bar to working for the BBC. He had a well earned reputation for bluntness that all too often deteriorated into rudeness. While acting as questionmaster on radio programmes like 'Round Britain Quiz' and 'Twenty Questions', he was constantly upsetting people and, on one occasion, was actually suspended from 'Twenty Questions' for losing his temper with the producer on the air. When he joined the 'What's My Line?' team, his main contribution was his predictable unpredictability. Viewers sat transfixed, trying to assess whether the quickening of his asthmatic wheeze meant mild irritation or signposted a coming explosion. When the eruptions came, the victim of his scorn was just as likely to be the shocked contestant as the hapless chairman, Eamonn Andrews.

With all the advance publicity and possibly her nervousness of the redoubtable Mr Harding, it was almost inevitable that Isobel's first appearance should come as something of an anti-climax. On Sunday 1 November, 1953, she sat alongside the unrepentant Gilbert Harding, the delightfully effervescent Barbara Kelly and another newcomer to the panel, the suave but nervous actor Michael Denison. Eamonn Andrews signed in a gemmologist, a sack-blower-up, a maker of sailor's trousers, a jetty carpenter, a photographic-finisher and a greyhound-track bookmaker. It was an inglorious debut, with Isobel so nervous she could not remember what questions had been asked by the other panellists, and she failed hopelessly in the bloodhound role.

She was far too intelligent not to realize that it had all gone wrong. If she had not been contracted to do another four programmes, she might have given up there and then. But again, it was Geoffrey who persuaded her to persevere despite the thumbs-down from some of the critics. At his insistence, she collected all the newspapers and sat poring over the various comments, looking for clues as to how she might improve her performance. But that did not work and her next three appearances proved to be little better than the first. She said later: 'I felt like an underwater swimmer who suddenly found himself thirty fathoms down in company with three sharks. It didn't matter that they were most helpful sharks who wouldn't have bitten a domesticated goldfish, they still looked like sharks. I suddenly realised that this was no happy-go-lucky show in the village hall, or an obscure broadcast with amateurs like myself. I was slap in the middle of a highly professional performance, with eight million people looking in and expecting to be entertained with the slick efficiency to which they had become accustomed. I have never been slick, efficiency is sadly lacking in my make-up and I'd never willingly entertained anyone in my life. Even family charades were for me anathema.'

There was no false modesty in that comment. It was, in fact, a piece of shrewd and honest self-assessment, which was underlined by the show's producer, Dicky Leeman. In his book, 'What's My Line?' published in 1955, he wrote: 'As she was the first to admit, she soon realised that airing your views in a discussion was one thing, and unravelling people's occupations in an apparently quite natural and effortless way was quite another.

'In "What's My Line?" Isobel Barnett found herself slap in the middle of Show Business, on one of the most controversial programmes ever put out by the BBC. She says she felt rather like a gold-fish swimming for her life, and under these circumstances, she simply could not relax, but sat in her place on the panel dreading her turn to face the camera.

'She also felt aware of all the glowing things that had been written about her after her first TV appearance on "Town Forum". She felt that she had been built up as "an unknown" from the provinces who would be sure to scintillate from the very start. When she failed to measure up to the expected standards, the critics, professional and amateur, proceeded to tear her to bits.'

She was 'trying too hard'. She was shy of 'letting her hair down'. 'Lady Barnett was as beautiful and intelligent as ever,' wrote a critic, 'but "What's My Line?" is quite obviously not the kind of programme in which she can be seen to the greatest advantage.' 'She might have thought she was back on the Bench,' wrote another.

When she read what some of the critics had to say, she may have wished she was back on the Bench. 'It's not the game it used to be,' said one writer, 'the new panel is not a success. It needs to be made up of four professional show people who have enough quick and natural wit to raise a laugh and to lift the often-jittery challengers out of their tongue-tied wariness. I would take out Lady Barnett, who is now clearly proved to be out of her depth.'

Isobel reluctantly endorsed that view: 'There is nothing more discouraging than to read something unpleasant about oneself, knowing it to be perfectly true. Lime Grove [where the show took place] and the dentist became synonymous for me. Everyone assured you there would be no pain, just relax and everything will be perfectly all right. Don't worry, it will all come out right in the end. It was just as untrue in the case of Lime Grove as it was of my dental visits.'

With one national newspaper already conducting a poll to find the most popular replacement for her, Isobel faced her last contracted appearance with something approaching relief, not only for herself but for Dicky Leeman who had so stoutly refused to be stampeded into sacking her earlier. When she left home that morning, Geoffrey had already gone off to play golf before the Sunday papers had arrived, but when one of his companions showed him the story about the poll, he abandoned his match and dashed off to try to catch Isobel at Leicester station. With ten minutes to spare before the train was due, he ushered her into the bleak refreshment room and gave her first a stiff drink and then a stiff talking to. He reminded her of her background and breeding and told her that ladies did not give up easily, if at all. Then he applied the charm, by assuring her how beautiful she was, and how clever, surely she would not allow a silly television programme to get the better of her when nothing else ever had? As she waved to him from the compartment window when the train pulled out, Isobel was in a much happier and almost belligerent mood.

At Lime Grove, she discovered that Dicky Leeman was conscious of it being St Andrew's Day and had booked mainly Scottish challengers. She at once felt at ease with the soft accents and was able to relax a little bit more. She also discovered that the growling Gilbert Harding was absent because of illness, and his place was to be taken by the irrepressible Robert Morley. Although the occasion became known to everyone connected with the show as 'Morley Night', it was also the night Lady Barnett came good. As she said later: 'I was so fascinated by Robert's antics that I forgot all about myself and my troubles. He

72

charged at the game like a bull in a china shop full of Crown Derby. He was brilliant, witty and brought a touch of outrageous comedy to the proceedings.' One of his questions, brought forth roars of laughter: 'Would I be right in assuming I'm wrong when I say . . .?' Isobel was still laughing when it was her turn to ask questions and to her astonishment she was, for the first time, getting positive answers and suddenly *knew* that the contestant must be a secretary. It was her first success. Dicky Leeman wrote: 'From that moment she never looked back. If I had sought to take her off the show a few weeks later, there would have been outbursts in the papers which a short while before had campaigned for her to be replaced. And they would have been quite right to shoot me down.'

The newspapers too changed their story. 'The BBC complains constantly of the shortage of talent. Well Lady Barnett is an argument for a more vigorous and discriminating search. Her charm, intelligence and poise have established her unassailably in the "What's My Line?" panel.' Another put it more succinctly: 'Lady Barnett has confounded the many critics who thought it would be her last appearance. For my money the Lady from Leicester, the beautiful amateur, is no longer the odd-girl out on a professional panel. She's show business.' He was, of course, quite right. Isobel was never inclined to do anything by half-measure and, with just as much dedication as she had showed in the early days of her medical training, she determined to learn as much as possible about what would be useful in her new career. Her teachers were the professionals of showbusiness – the performers, producers, cameramen, designers, technicians, and even those astute old guardians of a million secrets, the stage-doorkeepers. With a combination of charm and the ability to be a good listener (one of her special talents), she soaked up years of experience, albeit at secondhand. Her confidence grew daily and as it did, her performances on the screen became better and better. Within months, her popularity had soared and she had become a household name.

This was underlined by the massive publicity that attended her every move, and when, that same year, as an accolade to her new-found fame, she was invited to open the hugely popular Ideal Home Exhibition, the man who introduced her to the huge crowd told them: 'You feel as I do, that you know her already . . . she is one of the family.' But beyond that, both the public and the press showed an extraordinary naïvity in their attitude towards her. They expected their new heroine to be knowledgeable about everything under the sun, moreover they were willing to accept her opinions as readily as the ancients had listened to the word of the Oracle. When she had performed the opening ceremony at the exhibition, which was then regarded as the premier shopwindow for everything that was new in the building and furniture businesses, she was subjected to a long interview in which she was encouraged to lay down guidelines for other people looking for their ideal home. Luckily she had been chairman of her local council's housing committee and was therefore able to make realistic suggestions. The average family in 1954 should, she asserted, go for a modern house designed and equipped to save as much time and work as possible. If it had a garden – and she thought that essential – it should not be too large to be cared for properly. As to the then-current controversy over the vogue for a combined dining-sitting room, she diplomatically offered a compromise: a sitting room, with a dining recess. On furnishing, she said modern decoration and furniture were most suitable and stressed in particular the advantages of fitted wardrobes. For those who might not be able to afford proper fitted carpets, she recommended that they buy 'a good square and stain the surrounds.' As another economy measure, she advocated putting wallpaper on just one wall and using a contrasting paint on the other three. But she drew the line at messing around with new-fangled heating systems. She must have caused the electric and gas fire manufacturers to despair when she insisted that there was no substitute for a good, open coal fireplace.

Coal fires apart, she was painting a picture of how thousands of houses were to look in the mid-fifties, and her adoring fans were delighted that she should appear to underwrite their views. It did not matter to them that her own home reflected a entirely different set of tastes – a Georgian mansion with oak-blocked floors and fitted carpets; beautiful pastel-washed walls set off by expensive curtains and a collection of fine paintings; and a large garden ablaze with hundreds of different plants. Nor did it trouble them that her personal labour-saving was achieved by the employment of a housekeeper, two daily helps and a gardener!

But however gullible might have been the public, Isobel herself never lost sight of the danger in selling them short. One of the first things she learned was that however confident you might feel, you must never become blasé about making preparations for every appearance. For example, for 'What's My

Isobel at twenty-five, with
a very young Alastair.

Mother and son after
a day's riding.
Alastair is eight.

The Lord Mayor and Lady Mayoress of Leicester receiving guests at a reception in 1952.

The 'What's My Line?' panel in action, 1955. Left to right: David Nixon, Isobel Barnett, Barbara Kelly, Douglas Duff and chairman Eamonn Andrews. (*Popperfoto*)

Isobel visits the world's largest display of domestic textiles at the Royal Albert Hall, 1956. (*Popperfoto*)

Honorary Colonel of the WRAC, relaxing in the bar.

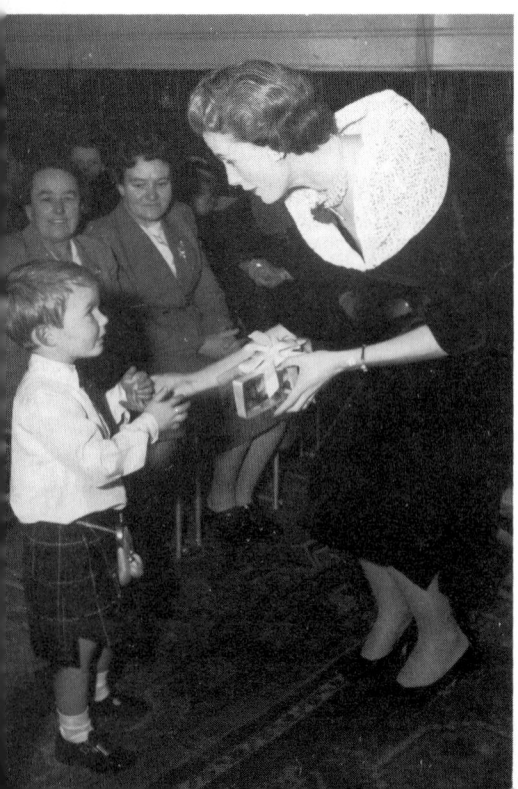

Receiving a presentation from
Molly Cox's son.

Line?' she acquired a list of twenty-three questions – from 'Do you give a service?' through 'Do you need special training?' to 'Can you do what you do for me?' – and always kept it by her in case she ever went blank.

At this distance, it is difficult to be certain why a programme like 'What's My Line?' should be so successful or why an unknown titled lady should gain such wide popularity. It may be that the reasons had more to do with what else was going on in Britain at the time. Post-war recovery had been a slower, more painful business than expected. Bread had been on ration until 1948; clothing coupons were needed until March 1950, when petrol also became more freely available; and soap was the last commodity to be de-rationed in September of that year. In fact, officially the state of war between Britain and Germany did not end until 1951 and by then the Korean trouble was threatening to erupt into another terrible world conflict. Britain was also suffering from political uncertainty. Mr Atlee's Labour Government was re-elected by such a small majority in 1950, that it survived only twenty months before Churchill led the Conservatives back to power with an equally uncomfortable majority.

Against such a grim backdrop, the infant, BBC-only television service must have been a welcome diversion for the few hours a day it was on the screen. Then, John Osborne was too young to give vent to his anger and the dramatists were still ignorant of the symbolism of the kitchen sink. Indeed, it was only radio's everyday story of 'The Archers' that had folk on the edge of their seats. The television programmes were a simple mixture of somewhat worthy studio-based discussions and a handful of escapist, light-entertainment shows.

While the critics paid more attention to the serious programmes, the viewers enjoyed the others, which gave them weekly glimpses of such glamourous acts as those high-kicking dancers, the Toppers. When 'What's My Line?' came along, it seemed to allow the audience to identify with the challengers and to have, each Sunday evening, the vicarious pleasure of rubbing shoulders with the stars. When Lady Barnett joined the panel, she seemed to open the door a little bit wider and viewers were then able to imagine they were seeing something of how the titled classes lived. Without any apparent envy, they enjoyed what they saw and Isobel took pleasure in her role as a bridge between the two worlds.

She also enjoyed the way people reacted to her public

appearances. Wherever she went she was mobbed by adoring fans. When she opened a new fashion store in Leeds, hundreds of women started queuing to see her more than three hours before she was due. In other towns they lined the streets and cheered as she drove by in her limousine. Despite the austerity of the times, there were bouquets and gifts at every turn and in many ways Isobel must have felt like royalty.

Being successful on television brought other rewards too, such as the opportunity to exploit other talents, and for Isobel, one of these was to write for the *Daily Sketch*. The editor gave her a whole page to write about her transformation from housewife to television star:

Everyone I meet asks the same questions: 'How do you feel about "What's My Line?" 'Do you enjoy it?' 'What's it like to be looked at by eight million people?' 'Are you nervous?' . . . 'Do you remember what it felt like to be a new girl at school?' That was how I felt the first night. The regular performers, especially Gilbert Harding, were very kind. But I was still terrified. It's bad enough to be a new girl, but it's worse still to know you are 'on appro'. I wasn't frightened of the viewers. Eight million people is rather like the National Debt – so vast that its past your comprehension. But I was frightened of the criticisms and comparisons that would be made between myself and my glamorous and talented predecessors. And I was afraid of the spotlight that beats on every detail of 'What's My Line?'.

Coming from complete obscurity to this programme in one fell swoop is a very big step. For the first few programmes I tried so hard. My brain worked overtime and I got nowhere. All my worst fears were realised. So I sat down and read the critics in the newspapers. They were far from flattering – but they were my greatest help because they turned me from a blue-stocking into a panellist. They taught me that it isn't only brains that are needed, but gaiety and a sense of fun. I took their advice – sat back, determined to enjoy myself, and hoped that the viewers would enjoy it, too. It's been fun ever since.

Instead of combing my hair back I decided to comb it forward to frame my face, because that way it didn't look nearly so hard and severe. In Bond Street I spotted a pair of chandelier ear-rings (you probably noticed that I was wearing them last week – and I lost one at a most vital moment in the middle of the programme) and I bought them because they seemed to be more eye-catching than the small ear-rings I had previously worn. I learnt a thing or two from the glamorous people I was mixing with!

Mind you, I'm still nervous before each programme. I can't settle down to anything at all on Sunday, before I leave home for London, I wander round doing my packing, trying to remember what I want to pack, and always forgetting something. But I think it's better that way.

If you are complacent you lose something vital – and your TV viewers soon know it!

'What's My Line?' of course is like a series of crossword puzzles. You have to get into a certain way of thinking and the more you practise the easier it becomes. But alas! The only way of practising properly is by practising on the viewers. Only then do you feel the real strain of concentrated thinking under a spotlight. If it were a sporting event I could best describe it as 'playing when the pressure is on'. It's a team game, and you learn to play together. It doesn't matter who actually nails the challenger's job because all the others have helped to pave the way.

I travel to London on Sunday mornings and stay with kind-hearted relations who put up with the coming in at all sorts of odd times to suit TV. When I get to the studio I go to the hospitality room with the panel and have a sherry. It helps to sweep the inhibitions away. And then we're on!

I rope my solicitor husband in most Sundays for a private 'What's My Line?' session, and he assumes the most improbable occupations. Last week, for instance, he decided to be a washerwoman – most difficult to guess when he told me that the job was 'fee earning'. Other times he has been easier to guess – he's been a golf caddie, a church verger, a window cleaner, a governess, a petrol filling station attendant and lots of other things.

Secretly he's tickled pink with my new job and he's also my sternest critic. When I return home he usually says. 'I am being ultra-critical, but . . .', and he points out the ways in which he thinks I could have been better. It's a great help.

Guessing jobs becomes almost an obsession after a few weeks on the panel, I find myself studying people in buses and trains and trying to guess what they do. Interest in the show is terrific and most encouraging. It takes me all my time to keep pace with viewer's letters.

Clothes, inevitably, are a real problem to feminine panellists since women viewers pay great attention to them. So many dresses are unsuitable. On television, when you're only seen as half a person, it's the necklines that matter. It's a particular problem for me as I live in the country and have little use for glamorous clothes here in Leicestershire. But I'm doing my best to compete with the stars of the panel. I manage to ring the changes with blouses and evening jerseys.

My life has been completely altered since I went into television, and it has all happened so quickly. But now I enjoy my two days a week in London, meeting so many new people and learning to talk a new (TV) language. It has jolted me out of a comfortable, industrious, serious rut to a new and exciting world.

Exciting as this new world might be, Isobel was sensible enough to know that she would not really enjoy it for very long if she did not keep her feet firmly on the ground, and she also knew the only place she would be likely to do that was at home, amid the ample acres of Leicestershire. She resisted the temptation to give up too many of her local activities and instead applied herself to a more careful apportionment of her time. After their year in office as Lord Mayor and Lady Mayoress, Geoffrey and she had become the deputies for a further year and thereafter still had a number of civic duties in the city. In addition, she was anxious to continue as a member of the rural district council and as a local magistrate. She also found time for a growing number of speaking engagements around the Midlands and, even before her 'What's My Line?' experience, had been establishing a reputation as a very good speaker.

Although she had no problems over Alastair because he was at boarding school, she did worry about Geoffrey. The combination of his civic responsibilities and increasing business interests were beginning to take a toll of his health and he was advised by his doctor to give up his ambitions to go into parliament. She persuaded him to give up as prospective Conservative candidate for the South Nottingham division and to cut back on some of his other work. She then found herself under some pressure to take his place as the candidate, but though, as a member of the party's national panel, she was always ready to speak in the Tory cause, she really had no personal ambitions to go into the House of Commons. Even if she had, at that particular time it would have been almost impossible for her to fit a hectic political campaign into her packed diary. In fact she was already having to employ a full-time secretary just to keep track of her movements – on one Saturday she could be at three or four fêtes in the afternoon and then at a dinner in the evening – and to deal with the growing number of letters from viewers.

Isobel was constantly surprised by the volume of response to her television appearances and sometimes shocked by the intensity of the letters. 'There are anonymous letters from those who hate you through and through,' she said, 'and I cannot see what satisfaction such missives give the writers, especially when they must know they are invariably burned without being fully read. But for every nasty letter, she received a hundred friendly messages and soon settled down to enjoying all the fuss and attention. She was particularly pleased that so many young people watched the programme and was delighted to be asked by them for autographs. She always told with great glee the story of one of her train journeys which was interrupted by a woman and two children coming into her compartment. 'I wonder if the children might each have your autograph?' asked the woman. 'I know it's an imposition, but they do so like you on the television.' Isobel assured her that it was no trouble at all and gaily signed her name with a flourish. But by the time she had finished signing there was little evidence of a flourish left. She had not realized that the woman was a teacher in charge of a school outing of 105 children, all of whom trooped in and out of the compartment. At the end of the marathon signing, Isobel apologized to the only other person in the compartment, an elderly and by now rather irritated gentleman. 'Well, madam,' he growled, 'I have no idea who you are, but as to what you are, I can only presume from your admirers that you are a lady footballer.'

When she was not signing 105 autographs or indulging in one of her favourite pastimes, talking to complete strangers on trains, Isobel often put her longer journeys to very good use. At home, she was always being interrupted by the telephone: on the train she was able to concentrate on making notes for her speaking engagements and public appearances or for responses to the ever-increasing number of press interviews. As the scenery and the miles sped by, she used the steady rhythm of the wheels to concentrate her mind and to focus her thoughts on a wide range of topics.

It was in handwriting made spidery by the swaying of the train that she first commented on the fledgling television service: 'I believe that television is man's greatest gift to women since invention began. It is another window in the home – in most cases the one with the finest view. And as the women of Britain are the home-makers, and spend most time there, television is both a blessing and a weapon for them. It can cheer their lonely hours, and it can help keep their families round them in the evenings.' But then, almost in defence of her own position in television, she asserted that women could be more than passive viewers: 'As a general rule, British men are even more shy and awkward before the television cameras than they are before the film cameras. But our girls are more quickly getting the feel of it. They have the advantage too, that not only do most men prefer to look at a woman on their home screen but so, also, do most women – albeit critically in some cases. It's probably the eternal instinct in us to watch and learn from others of our sex. At any rate it would seem so from the letters I receive each week about my ear-rings, my hair-style and my dress.' She had obviously had some letters about wearing a low-cut dress and, in a hasty scribble, worked out her justification: 'I do it naturally, mainly to ring the changes in the way that any woman would. Sometimes it probably seems lower-cut than it is because the camera is higher than normal eye-level. This isn't easy to guess in advance, but I really do deplore the trick of wearing too little just to catch the camera. I do believe that the frequent emphasis on 'cleavage' (as low-cut necklines are called there) in America is harmful to television, and to the women who play it that way.'

On other journeys she put together notes of some of her likes and dislikes: 'My greatest dislike in life is the man who gets me on the telephone through his secretary – and then he can't be found. You have to hang on for several valuable minutes quite unfairly and unncessarily.' She obviously warmed to the task of releasing some of her irritations because she added in a barely legible scribble: 'I dislike people who are ashamed of their families – people who are ashamed to acknowledge their beginnings. The great difference between the Scots and the English is that the Scots don't have the same class consciousness. They don't have to be rude to prove it. They don't have to be aggressive or show off to keep up their ego.' And being, as she saw herself, a classless Scot, she hated snobs: 'I hate people who put on a tremendous show. I would rather be asked into the kitchen in sincerity than into the drawing-room for show.'

All that is left of her likes are two tiny notes: 'I like being up early in the morning – once I am up. I dislike the thought of getting up before I'm up. But once I'm up it's a different story – I really love it.' And, more surprisingly: 'I like circuses, and roundabouts of every description, with the noise and the lot. I think I should have been born into a circus.'

The millions who watched 'What's My Line?' would never have guessed it, but in those early days, Lady Barnett faced every show in fear and trepidation. All her life she had been concerned with keeping up appearances and, as she later admitted, she was scared stiff of making a fool of herself. What the television audience saw was someone who looked and acted every bit the lady, always calm and controlled. Not even when her mother died – in February 1954 – did anyone see the faintest faltering. Indeed, it would have been very easy to get the impression that she was cold and uncaring. She cancelled only one appearance on the programme, to go to Glasgow for the funeral. A few days later, she was back in London for the following week's edition, as cheerful and witty as ever, just as if nothing had happened. It may be that her medical training had helped her to accept death. When, in her student days she had seen her first dead body, she said she then understood death as a natural phenomenon rather than as some great spiritual disaster. But could she have maintained such clinical detachment over her own mother's death?

Perhaps a more likely explanation for the outward lack of feeling is that beneath her overt gregariousness, Isobel was such an intensely private person that she could not share with anyone the darker, more uncomfortable emotions. There is some evidence for this suggestion in her autobiography published the year after her mother's death. Although the book, *My Life Line*, is dedicated: 'To my mother, who only saw the beginning,' there is not a single word about her death, let alone a comment on how Isobel might have felt. Nor does she let show her reactions to any of the events that might be expected to have caused her distress. Her only brother's death in childhood is given three lines. She was a little more forthcoming about her father's death, and recalled how badly the news had been broken to her. But again nothing about how she *felt* about his death. Even her first love, the young doctor who let her down by going out with other girls, is allocated only one sentence: 'I don't remember if he ever passed his surgery finals and, after the blow his duplicity had given my emotional ego, I really didn't care very much.' But it has to be said that even when she obviously did care very much, you still could not tell. By anyone's standards, three months from first meeting to marriage must represent a whirlwind courtship and two people head-over-heels in love, but you would not guess that from Isobel's account: 'Captain Barnett was being most attentive. He was now stationed at the War Office in London, but had managed to come up to Glasgow to see me on two occasions, but our courtship was conducted under every kind of difficulty. The Blitz was at its height and trunk calls were erratic and often took several hours to come through. I could only take his calls in the resident's sitting-room, my ward, or the corridor of the nurses' home. In any of these spots it was very difficult to carry on any conversation that could be called romantic. I must have been a most guarded and unsatisfactory telephonic lover. But if these conversations were completely unsatisfactory for the two chief participants they provided a lot of quiet amusement for others. If I answered from my ward, the old ladies would arouse themselves from the deepest of slumbers to listen to the doctor talking to her "young man".

They adored every moment, and I'm sure it helped their convalescence.'

There is no mention at all of the early illness of her son, Alastair, although it was serious enough to cause her to give up the work that she loved so much; nor of her husband's health problems, although they were bad enough to force him to abandon his political ambitions.

It is possible, of course, that these ommissions were accidental. The book is very busy, packed with lovely anecdotes, and it could be that Isobel did not notice she had skated over these important events. But when one reads a passage about her reluctance to get involved in the university's many organizations, there's further evidence that she probably did not want to write about them: 'I did get inveigled into attending one Oxford Group meeting, but came away shocked and disturbed by the public confessions of sins great and small. I am all for confession as practised by Catholics, and can imagine the wonderful spiritual comfort and relief it must bring. But then it is practised in decent privacy, shared only by a priest, who is full of an understanding and compassion for the shortcomings of his flock, and who in the light of his profession can grant absolution and forgiveness to a tortured soul. But to listen to this avowal of petty sin before total strangers was too much for me. I felt they might just as well have removed all their clothes in public.'

But if it is a long way from today's brutally revealing self-portraits, Isobel's autobiography does offer some insights into her personality. She writes about her cosseted childhood, the family servants, about being a debutante and about her own academic achievements – all as if she thought this was the norm and she was Little Miss Average. When she was first reported as being a new member of the 'What's My Line?' panel and there was the press discussion about her title, she could not understand what all the fuss was about: 'If I had been Mrs Barnett nobody would have dreamed of addressing me as such. I should have been Isobel Barnett automatically. But that little word "Lady" appeared to make a vast difference. This distrust of titles has fascinated me. Why you should be any different because you change your name I cannot imagine. Yet that "Lady" haunts me. Things you did or did not do when you were plain Mrs take on a new significance when you are Lady. If I can't attend a bazaar or fête because of another engagement the reaction seems to be, "Oh well, I suppose she has no time for us now that she's Lady Barnett." Far from being the asset it is supposed to be, a title is a liability.'

Isobel was, in fact, very conscious that the title was only hers by courtesy of her husband's knighthood and was a stickler about its proper use. She was perfectly happy to be called simply by her Christian name and invariably introduced herself as just 'Isobel Barnett', never allowing anyone to get away with 'Lady Isobel', the style correctly used only by ladies with titles in their own right.

What is also apparent in the book, is her resentment of what she regarded as unfair criticism of both herself and the programme: 'One TV critic writing of my appearance in "What's My Line?" wrote, "There sat Lady Barnett, every inch the efficient bazaar-opener." Quite frankly I do not wish to spend thirty out of fifty-two Saturdays opening anything, but I feel it is part of the job and a way of repaying a debt of gratitude to the public, who have generously given me so much kindness. I *am* an efficient bazaar-opener through long practice, and I don't care if I look like one on "What's My Line?" or anywhere else. Yet another critic wrote of me, "If Lady Barnett coos good evening to every challenger I shall scream" – or words to that effect. Yet if I don't say "good evening", I get a spate of letters from irate mothers who chide me for my lack of politeness. These differences of opinion do keep the panellist on both horns of dilemma.'

Of the programme, she felt an even stronger need for justification:

I have for some time been at a loss to understand why so many of the critics appear to have marked antipathy to 'What's My Line?' when the game is obviously so enjoyed by the public. There are, after all, few shows which can be watched with equal enjoyment by the seven-year-old and the seventy-year-old, and by people from every walk of life from the ducal palace to the condemned tenement block.

One critic told me that his reason for disliking the game was that he was so infuriated that anything so puerile should have such a hold on the public, and that is possibly the attitude of his colleagues. But surely that is the attitude of Canute who forbade the sea to advance another inch. 'What's My Line?' appeals to certain very basic and human qualities present in all of us, and in that lies its success.

Firstly it brings to the screen ordinary men and women from town and village doing something they do every day of their lives. There's no act about it, they are perfectly natural, and viewers can identify themselves with them. The plumber looking in can view his fellow plumber on the screen, criticize his mime, and shout with rage at his evasive answers.

Then there is the appeal of knowing more than the so-called experts. For five minutes everyone in Britain knows the challenger's job and we do not. They can sit in their armchairs watching us struggle and squirm. They can join in the game, saying, 'Oh, go on, Gilbert – there, I knew he'd get it, he always does,' or they can wriggle in their chairs exclaiming, 'For heaven's sake ask him if he works outside.' It's all very human and absolutely harmless.

The same, however, could not be said of the searing glare of stardom to which Isobel found herself subjected. The intensity of the spotlight was clearly having its effect when, with uncharacteristic bitterness, she wrote:

Until quite recently I was painfully vulnerable to the opinions of other people. Being unsure of myself and very aware of my own shortcomings, it used to fill me with deep depression to know that someone thought ill of me. It did not matter in the least that that person was somebody for whom I had no respect and whose opinion was valueless to me, I still felt his censure deeply and still retained a deep sensitivity to criticism.

But, whenever you achieve a coveted and envied position, even in any stratum of society, then that position, however lowly, lays you wide open to criticism from all sides. The criticism may be unfair and unjust. The one who criticises probably could not do any better than you are doing, but by becoming president of the Mothers' Union or head stamp-licker in the Post Office, you must be prepared to be torn to pieces in public and in private. But if you can take it, then sooner or later you acquire a philosophy and the criticism ceases to wound because you suddenly realise that each individual has his own standards, and they are the only ones which are of any significance in life.

Each of us is his own judge and jury. We have got to live with our own private conscience, and praise from the public is dust and ashes compared with your private shame if you fail to follow the dictates of that nagging conscience. A life-time of criticism is worth while if you stick to the principles you believe to be the right ones.

If for no other reason than my emancipation from the slings and arrows of outrageous fortune I should have counted my TV life as worth while.

However, as was to become sadly obvious nearly twenty-five years later, she was being less than prophetic when she added: 'Thanks to the publicity of a television life, I have made one discovery that a more sensible woman would have made long before now, a discovery which saves me for all time from the barbs and pricks of harsh criticism. I have, through necessity, become impervious to what gossip has to say about me.'

It is not at all clear to what she was referring in this last comment. Apart from the initial scepticism about her early appearances on 'What's My Line?', she attracted little criticism and certainly nothing that could be called harsh ever appeared in print. On the contrary, she had become the darling of the press and few television personalities can ever have received so much flattery over the years. No doubt she received the odd spiteful letter or bitchy remark from jealous acquaintances, but these were massively countered by compliments. It could be that she was already rehearsing her earlier suggestion of being her own judge and jury – a dual role that was later to have such tragic consequences.

CHAPTER 9

Once the popularity bandwagon started rolling for Lady Barnett, it seemed nothing could stop it – not that she would have let anything impede her progress anyway. From the moment she decided that television was going to be her career for at least the foreseeable future, she committed herself to it as surely as she had to her medical training. She concentrated first on getting the performance right and was delighted to find that her old skill in diagnosing patients' illnesses could be adapted to fathoming out what the 'What's My Line?' challengers did for a living. Her carefully acquired bedside-manner also came in handy for putting other people at their ease and her amazing memory helped her keep track of all the other panellists' questions. Once she was reasonably satisfied that she was meeting her own standards, she turned her attention to her appearance and then to ironing out the last vestiges of her Glasgow accent. The end result was an overtly confident, stylish professional who, although the description had not then been coined, was fast becoming one of television's first superstars. Wherever she went, she was mobbed by enthusiastic fans. On one occasion so many people crowded into a London store where she was signing copies of her book that the worried manager had to ask her to leave early for fear that the floor would collapse under the unexpected weight. It reached the stage where she would only sign autographs with her back to a secure wall because of the danger of being over-run. She had become public property.

She was at first amused by the constant interest in everything she did, but became irritated when her clothes and general appearance began to merit critical attention in the fashion press. She never had any pretentions to be a particularly well dressed woman, let alone to be a leader of fashion. She enjoyed shopping for clothes and was always careful to buy good quality, well cut suits and dresses, but beyond that she was uninterested.

Nor was it only in the subject of fashion that she was expected to be an expert. In her new public persona, the press felt entitled to ring her up and ask for her views on anything from the death penalty to free school milk, or for advice to their readers on how to hold down a job and look after a family at the same time. With opinions it was easy. Isobel had a view about everything and was always happy to have the chance to develop her arguments, although on the practical front she was not exactly the best person to ask for advice. If she had been completely honest she would probably have said the best thing to do would be to find a good housekeeper, just as she had always done. Instead, she evaded the request for advice and offered another piece of Barnett philosophy: 'A certain amount of method is necessary if a house is going to be well run, but I think the secret of enjoying housekeeping is to let method and routine remain as virtues, rather than to become instead deadly vices. It's so easy when you are a housewife to become the slave of habit rather than its mistress. Does the happiness of the home really depend upon turning out the dining-room without fail on Tuesdays? Must the kitchen floor be scrubbed meticulously twice a week?

I go on the happy supposition that so long as the house is warm, reasonably clean and welcoming, so long as there is plenty of good food, and Geoffrey has mended socks and shirts with their full quota of buttons, I can go out as the spirit moves me to see something of the world outside the four walls of home.'

It was what went on *inside* her four walls that intrigued the producers of the BBC series 'At Home', who asked if they could do one of their programmes from the White House. Unaware of what it would entail or that the previous week's host had been Peter Ustinov, Isobel asked Geoffrey if he minded. He did not, he assured her, and even thought it might be 'quite good fun'. What neither of them realized was that the programme was done as a live outside broadcast – one of the most complex and time-consuming forms of television. It took nearly a month to set up, and the beautiful house and garden were virtually transformed into a studio, with cameras, lighting and all the other paraphernalia of broadcasting, fed by miles of umbilical cord from the huge technical vehicles parked outside in the village's one and only main street. With all that in the background, it must have been very difficult for the Barnetts to then fulfil the brief of the programme – to be their normal selves, going about their normal domestic life. After the programme had gone out – with only one small hitch when someone put on the wrong gramophone record and left Isobel talking about Chopin against a background of Brahms – the audience reaction was amazing. Young Alastair received nearly fifteen pounds of sugar lumps for his pony, Titmouse, from little girls all over the country and fourteen of them wanted to be pen pals. The family's pet poodle, Anna, was made an honourary member of the Tail-Waggers Club and was sent a badge to prove it. Isobel's secretary was inundated with offers and sales brochures for office stationery and equipment. A nursery gardener sent twelve chrysanthemum cuttings because, he said, the best part of the programme was the look on the gardener's face when Isobel was trying to take one cutting herself. And the letters poured in, at the rate of nearly two hundred a day, from viewers who all said they were delighted to have been allowed to join Lady Barnett and her family 'At Home'. For their part, Lady Barnett and her family had thoroughly enjoyed having guests, but were never more relieved than when they all left.

From the little village in Leicestershire, the bandwaggon rolled on, gathering pace and sweeping Isobel into more and more television work. Between 'What's My Line?' sessions, she became a presenter and interviewer on the afternoon programmes for women. She found the second role very much easier than the first. She had always been a very good listener and, as a doctor, had developed the technique for asking questions to elicit information people often did not know they had. Television interviewing, she said, was really only a variation of the diagnostician's role. But presenting the programme was a very different matter. She had a very poor memory for names, and in those days, there were no teleprompters to help her. Her fear of forgetting who she was supposed to be introducing almost became a phobia and she was driven to trying all the allegedly foolproof methods of memory-jogging. Everytime she met someone new, she followed the American psychologist's advice to repeat their name at least three times in every sentence within the first ten minutes of conversation. It was not successful. Strangers baulked at this apparent over-familiarity and the sensitive Lady Barnett shied away from being thought gushing. She fell back on the older association-of-ideas routine, until the day she called one unfortunate man Mr Balham instead of Mr Clapham. She knew he had the same name as a railway junction, but could not remember which one.

Ironically, it was the interview and not the presentation that almost floored her in the very first programme. Her first 'victim' turned out to be an old man who was very hard of hearing and who over-compensated for that deificiency by talking non-stop. For five very long minutes, the elegant Lady Barnett perspired under the studio lights as the man ignored her every question and just went rattling on as if she was not there. Even worse, she saw the funny side of it very early in the so-called interview and had to contain herself from bursting out laughing. It might have been the end of a short career if her next interviewee had not been Kenneth Horne, who bubbled and sparkled so naturally that the conversation was over before she realized it. She was back on the rails and from then on never had any difficulty in interviewing, whether it was the man in the street or, as on one occasion, Bertrand Russell.

The next challenge for Lady Barnett came with the BBC's launching of consumer programmes on television. She was invited to take part in a new series called 'Look and Choose' which, in the 1950s was innovative in that it made very frank assessments of everything that a woman might buy for the home. The idea had arisen from a national survey which had shown that many women were bad shoppers and had little notion of what to look for, tending to think that the most expensive article was always the best. The irony of choosing Isobel, whose own early experiences of shopping could have outdone any of the survey's most pathetic cases, was sadly lost on the producers. And to be fair, she had improved a little!

At this stage, it would have been easy for Isobel to abandon completely her old way of life and become a full-time television professional. She was in constant demand and could have taken her pick of a wide range of work. Instead, she resisted many of the offers to ensure that she had time at home, especially whenever Alastair was on holiday from boarding school. With his political interests curtailed – he finally retired from the city council in 1956 – Sir Geoffrey was widening his business activities, and Isobel played an important role in entertaining his new associates. As always, she proved a wonderful listener at dinner parties and picked up so much information in the process that she became almost as keen as her husband in playing the stock market, developing into an astute investor. She also found time to search for antiques that would fit into their beautiful Georgian home and to supervise work in the exquisite gardens.

It is true to say that, although he did not quite fit into the new showbusiness world his wife had discovered, Sir Geoffrey was very pleased with her success and he accompanied her whenever possible, to the various functions. He had the older man's special pride in his beautiful young wife and was astonishingly tolerant of her career's interference with his more sedate life-style. He was very much the formal, business figure in his dark suits, and sometimes looked out of place on occasions such as garden fêtes and bazaars. Whenever she caught him looking awkward or slightly lost, Isobel would gently persuade him to go away and get a cup of tea or some other refreshments while she got on with whatever business was expected of her. But if he was in the background – in her shadow – in public, it was quite different in private. Everyone who knew them was aware that Sir Geoffrey really was the head of the family and that that was the way Isobel liked it. From the early days of their marriage she had relied on him in countless ways, to the extent that she was quite dependent on him. He was always her sheet-anchor and she hated being away from him for any longer than necessary. Wherever she went on her travels across the United Kingdom, she always tried to get back to Leicestershire at night. She also relied on him as a sounding-board for her ideas and as a source of advice and comfort in the day-to-day problems of being a television star.

She did not, however, need anyone's advice about whether or not to accept the offer of a part in a Pinewood Studios film. She accepted immediately when they told her the film, 'Simon and Laura', would star Kay Kendall and Peter Finch. She and her co-pannelist from 'What's My Line?', Gilbert Harding, were to play themselves by way of providing a realistic background to the story of a theatrical couple who play out their domestic bliss for the television audience.

When the script arrived, Isobel, in her usual way, put off learning her lines until the last possible moment – on this occasion, the day before she was due at Pinewood. It was her first taste of learning lines since her schooldays and she did not find it easy. On her way to the studios at six o'clock the next morning, she was still very unsure of herself, as she admitted in her autobiography:

As with any new experience, I was petrified and wondered if I dare get lost on the drive and never turn up at all. Strangling that cowardly notion before it could take effect, I drove into the studios.

After a prolonged make-up which left me looking like a startled fawn with the doe-eyed look, and a visit to hair-dressing, I was collected and delivered on to a set which was a replica of Raymond's beautiful salon – a symphony of pink and grey and complete to the last detail. Our little scene consisted of a girlish exchange of confidences amongst the hair-dryers and glossy magazines. The scene was to last only two minutes in the film, but we took three hours to shoot it!

Feeling uncomfortably aware that I was no Rin-Tin-Tin or Shirley Temple, I crept forward, but my apprehensions vanished when I met the producer of the film, Muriel Box, and the star, Kay Kendall. They couldn't have been kinder.

I found to my relief that nobody cared too much about the script. It wasn't nearly so rigid as the Lady Macbeth variety. So long as you kept things in the proper order, sounded natural, and tossed out the correct cues, that was as much as anyone expected.

The scene was rehearsed, rehearsed and then rehearsed again with enormous attention to detail, and then finally we were ready for the first take. Alarm bells jangled suddenly and I wondered what had got on fire, only to discover that was the signal for all doors to be hermetically sealed, leaving us safely shut in until the scene was completely filmed. Then, with clappers clanging before our eyes, we were off on Scene 12, Take 1. This procedure was repeated time and time again as the scene was shot from every angle . . . . which I found very confusing, used as I was to the freedom of the TV set. I was suddenly told: 'You must hold your cigarette in your left hand, not your right one, and don't put down that magazine until Miss Kendall says "Isobel". 'The same lines had to be repeated over and over again for each take, until you were sick of the sound of them and they sounded banal and meaningless.

This was my first experience of doing anything which required rehearsal. For the TV programmes, so long as I said what was necessary and confined my remarks to a given number of seconds or minutes I could vary them as much as I liked at each run-through and we never had two runs-through alike.

After the morning's filming, which made me realise that a film star's life is not all mink coats, orchids, and film premieres, but really hard work, we adjourned for luncheon. Dress at lunch was cheerfully varied. We all wore oddly coloured make-up and a startling mixture of clothes. Kay Kendall was lunching in a hairdresser's smock, Muriel Pavlov looked like a charmingly pretty refugee from behind the Iron Curtain, while David Tomlinson was wearing a violently striped pair of flannel pyjamas as though he wore that every day and lunched in nothing else.

I enjoyed my day's filming, but when I attended the film premiere, I found it an unnerving and eerie experience to see myself on the screen. It's bad enough to catch sight of yourself suddenly in a mirror in an hotel or a ballroom, but that is mild compared with seeing and hearing yourself in Vistavision and full Technicolor. It filled me with a deep sense of relief that, as all the shows I have done on TV are live programmes and are never filmed, I have never had an opportunity to see myself as others see me except on this one fleeting occasion.

How others saw Lady Barnett was as an accomplished and seasoned performer who could be relied on to be very good at absolutely everything she turned her hand to. She popped up everywhere on radio and television, as an interviewee or guest on programmes from Jeanne Heal's show to radio's 'Twenty Questions,' delighting audiences with a combination of wit and common sense. After her initial uncertainties, she was never again at a loss for words – the perfect professional who always turned up having done her homework and prepared for any eventuality.

This total and awesome competence was reflected in her private life and her close friend, Norah Cheatle, could say without the slightest hint of resentment, that she saw her as something of a paragon. 'You couldn't talk about a piece of music that she didn't know something about, because she listened to her records so much. And, of course, she was so succcessful at everything that I felt a bit of a nit alongside her. But she never pushed her knowledge, it always emerged as a natural part of her conversation.' Such paragons invariably attract a certain degree of bitchiness, but Lady Barnett escaped most of that according to Mrs Cheatle: 'She was never critical of anyone. She always saw the good in people and that's what everyone saw in her, even though she did overshadow us most of the time. Our little social group was always well dressed and when we gathered for some special occasion we usually felt we looked pretty smart – until Isobel turned up looking immaculate!'

She had not always been immaculate. At school and university she had appeared quite ordinary. Her plump figure had not lent itself to smartness and although her clothes were expensive, her friends say she had no real dress sense. That came later, as part of Sir Geoffrey's carefully-contrived grooming exercise. He drummed into her, so consistently, the need to look exactly right that it became almost an obsession to strive for perfection.

This near-perfection became Lady Barnett's stock-in-trade and her secretary, Jeanne Burton, says friends were always relieved and delighted when her arrangements went slightly haywire. She tells the story of one Christmas when Lady Barnett was preparing a traditional, but elaborate, lunch with turkey and all the trimmings, for some very distinguished guests. The first people had already arrived and were enjoying a pleasant drink when Mrs Burton suddenly noticed that the oven, in which the turkey should have been turning a golden brown, was not working. In the middle of the panic, another couple of guests arrived and the truth was blurted out. 'Oh goodie!' said the titled lady, 'I thought nothing ever went wrong in this household.' From then on, the occasion was more successful than ever.

The army spotted Lady Barnett's talents, and in a very smart piece of recruiting they made her Honorary Colonel of a WRAC. Territorial Army battalion which had troops in Leicester, Northampton and Peterborough. She took the appointment very seriously and as soon as she joined up, she joined in, involving herself in the wide range of their activities from evening drill sessions, through regular riding with the battalion's Saddle Club to the annual two-week camp. She looked impeccable in the dark green uniform and seemed to revel in the *camaraderie* of the Other-Ranks' Club as much as she enjoyed the style of the Officers' Mess.

It was this ability to find an easy rapport with people of all classes that made so many of Isobel's public appearances – and they were increasing in regularity all the time – so much fun for everyone concerned. When she visited a bedding factory in Derbyshire she bounced on the bed and swapped saucy stories with the factory-hands; when she attended a businessmen's banquet she delighted the industrialists with her knowledge of how much their shares were worth. And wherever she went, the press were in attendance to keep their readers informed of her every move. Her readiness to answer questions and be generally cooperative made her a favourite with journalists and led to hundreds of articles being published about her over the years. One of the best appeared in 1959 in the *John Bull Illustrated*, written by Rex Grizell: 'In the world of entertainment, Lady Barnett is unique. She does not sing, dance or tell amusing stories. She is not a musician, an actress, an archaeologist, or even a political expert. She is never rude, provocative or bad-tempered. Her television personality has been based on a nice smile, an occasional pensive frown, a form of studied politeness which sometimes verges on condescension and a wide selection of ear-rings. Yet in a few short years, Isobel Morag Barnett, five feet nine inches tall and nine stone-plus of inexorable charm, has become a national institution as difficult to explain to a visitor from abroad as other British mysteries, like cricket and public schools.'

But it's when the article turns to the Barnetts' husband-and-wife relationship that the reader has the strongest flavour of Lady Barnett's own John Bull characteristic: 'When she was chairman of her rural district housing committee, Sir Geoffrey was chairman of the much more powerful Leicester housing committee. "My husband wanted to grab half our land for a new housing estate. I decided to fight him tooth and nail," she says. Lady Barnett won.'

Rex Grizell also took note of Isobel's domestic image: 'As a keen businesswoman she has not neglected to take advantage of her casting as the perfect mother. In radio programmes and newspaper articles she has told the Mrs Browns of the world how to run a home, how to keep a husband and how to bring up children. As a rule she comes down on the side of the husbands. "The only logical husband-and-wife arrangement is for the man to make the woman an allowance, not the other way round. To me a husband in an apron is a lamentable sight. Wives who coax or nag their men always to help with the washing up, for shoe cleaning or the fires are undermining a man's whole character." Sir Geoffrey comments undestandably: "I really can't think of anything about Isobel that isn't thoroughly nice." He prefers not to discuss his wife's public life. When Features (Cossington) Limited was formed it was Sir Geoffrey who changed the wording of the memorandum expressing the company's purpose from "the promotion for commercial purposes of the name and reputation of Isobel Morag Barnett in all parts of the world" to the "promotion of entertainment for commercial purposes in all parts of the world." It sounded nicer.'

Typically, Lady Barnett was desperately anxious to keep everything in perspective and she ended the interview with the comment that no one but herself believed: 'It's nice being picked out as a somebody but of course I know I don't deserve it. I have no talent.'

CHAPTER 10

With her quite remarkable determination to keep her private self as firmly under wraps as possible, it is not especially easy to see just what effect being catapulted into the nerve-jangling confusion of showbusiness had on Lady Barnett. She was so adept in the middle-class art of emotional self-defence that she was able to give the impression of taking everything in her stride.

She never lost her anxiety about what other people thought about her and so carefully set about reconstructing her image to meet the expectations of the 'What's My Line?' audience and of the press. Mindful of what she regarded as the cruel taunts of the fashion-writers, she began to dress with a touch more flamboyance. She lowered her neckline and matched Barbara Kelly ear-ring for dangling ear-ring. She experimented with make-up and became more adventurous in her hair styles. Sir Geoffrey played an important role in her re-grooming, just as he had done in her earlier transition from bouncy young Scottish graduate to sophisticated county-setter, and his encouragement gave her the confidence to laugh more readily and to contrive to deepen even further her already rich brown voice. But impressive as the end result might have been, not even her husband's constant support could protect her completely from the stresses and strains of living in a goldfish bowl. As she worked on her appearance with all the skill of the artist using a palette knife to mix just the right shade, what she was really doing was covering up some of the private cracks caused by the relentless pressure of staying at the top in the competitive world of television.

There was, of course, no pretence about whether or not she enjoyed being a star. She quite simply and unashamedly loved it and, although she often commented on its ephemeral and superficial nature, it was in television she found the kind of heart-pounding excitement for which she had longed while still at university. The buzz of high tension in the studio just before the red transmission light went on always caused a great surge of adrenalin in her and that, she said, was when she felt most alive.

Nor could there be any doubt about her delight in the opportunity to rub shoulders with the famous. Unlike so many celebrities, she never became blasé about moving in star-studded circles. Indeed, name-dropping was one of her favourite pastimes. It had always been one of her weaknesses: at' school and university, she used the names of her father's most eminent medical colleagues to impress her friends, and later, when talking to local government associates in Leicestershire, she sprinkled the conversation with the names of judges she had met as Lady Mayoress. Her move into television instantly multiplied her circle of famous acquaintances: not only did she regularly appear with Eamonn Andrews, Barbara Kelly, Gilbert Harding and David Nixon, but every week she added another 'scalp' through the celebrity challengers.

One of the main drawbacks for Isobel, however, was that the hectic pace of her new lifestyle precluded the natural development of any fresh relationships much beyond the acquaintance level while, at the same time, it inevitably distanced her from many of her old friends. The more long-standing of these – like Molly Spencer, who had since married and become Mrs Cox – understood the situation and were more than happy with the odd scribbled note, a hurried telephone call or the occasional meeting. 'It was always fun when Isobel did get in touch,' said Molly. 'She had a tremendous facility for making you feel you were the most important person to her at that moment. She could always concentrate totally on whoever she was with at any time and although we all knew how very busy she was, she never seemed in a hurry when she was actually with you. The name-dropping never bothered me because she never put on any airs or graces or talked about her own celebrity status.'

Isobel valued her old friends and as she moved inexorably to the centre of the public stage, she had to work twice as hard to protect her relationships and her privacy. This undoubtedly caused some strain, the signs of which were most obvious when she was on holiday, well away from the bright lights. For several years, she, Geoffrey and young Alastair had continued to visit Tenby for their summer break and had always stayed in the same rooms in the same seafront hotel, the Atlantic, run by Mrs

Pauline Rees. She recalls that in the early years, from around the time when they were Lord Mayor and Lady Mayoress of Leicester, they were the ideal guests. Geoffrey, quiet and reserved, was the perfect gentleman whose good manners impressed everyone; Isobel, extrovert and friendly, had an infectious gaiety that made her very popular with other guests; and young Alastair was a bright little lad, who mixed happily with the children in the hotel. The family became friendly with a couple from Cheshire, a retired Royal Navy surgeon-commander and his wife, and they used to go back to the hotel together for the same two weeks each year. It all meant for happy, relaxed holidays.

Mrs Rees said things began to change when Lady Barnett became so popular on television. She seemed less happy mixing with other people and was only really comfortable with her own small group of friends. She was always the leader of the group and her animated conversation sometimes descended into noisy garrulity. The group would often commandeer the hotel's only lounge, and it would be Isobel, fiercely protective of her clique, who froze out the other guests. Then they took to going out for midnight bathing parties and waking everyone else up when they came noisily back in the small hours. They were not exactly rowdy, just thoughtless, but there is no doubt, according to Mrs Rees, that the other guests became tired of their behaviour and when some of them began talking about cancelling their bookings for the following year, she decided that it was the Barnetts who she would rather not have again. When Lady Barnett's secretary later phoned to book, she simply said the rooms were not available at the time they wanted. Lady Barnett would, of course, be highly sensitive to such a rebuff and obviously understood the implicit message because she never went back to Tenby.

At home in Leicestershire there were also signs of strain as her television and public appearances increased. Something had to suffer and inevitably it was her local government work. She found it more and more difficult to get to meetings of the rural district council and one year was embarrassed to find herself bottom of the list for attendance. Of the thirty council and committee meetings she should have been at, she managed only eight. She was very quick to apologize: 'The difficulty is that by the time I get the dates for all the meetings, I'm often booked up professionally,' she explained. Again, however, she showed some resentment about the implied criticism in any question about her engagements: 'The villagers still elect me though they know my limitations. If they find me too unsatisfactory, they have their remedy.' It has to be said that the electors did seem perfectly happy and the council clerk made it clear that a little of Lady Barnett was better than no Lady Barnett at all. 'We don't mind a bit,' he said, 'we're glad she has stayed with us. She is such a useful member.'

At that particular time, Lady Barnett was not only serving on the council but she was also a magistrate, an honorary colonel in the WRAC, a governor of the British Film Institute, president of the district NHS Reserve, president of the local branch of the Spastics Society and patron or vice-president of more than a dozen other Midland charities and voluntary organizations. There is not the shadow of doubt that anyone from any of the groups with which she was involved would have said the same as that council clerk: for them, an occasional visit from the golden Lady Barnett was more stimulating and more encouraging than full-time support from most other people. Whenever she did appear, she gave of herself completely and each group could, with some justification, feel that it was the most important on her circuit.

It was the same in her professional life. She never missed a performance of 'What's My Line?' (other than the one which coincided with the death of her mother) and when she was at the Television Theatre, where the show was recorded, she played a key role in making both the challengers and the celebrity guests feel equally at their ease. She travelled all over Britain to open bazaars and fêtes and every kind of money-raising function and never seemed in a hurry. She would allow herself to be guided around every little stall or sideshow and to be shaken by the hand by every voluntary worker or clapped on the back by enthusiastic members of the public. In her lecturing and after-dinner speaking, which she had shrewdly turned into a flourishing business, she was always good value. She prepared herself very well, locking herself in her study to prepare notes – nearly always at the last minute. She spoke off the cuff, seldom even referring to the careful notes, and laced every talk with wit and humorous anecdote. Randolph Churchill, not exactly renowned for his generosity of spirit, heard one of her after-dinner speeches and sent her his place-card with a little note on the back saying it was the best he had ever heard, 'from either sex.' Over the years, she collected hundreds of similar tributes and developed a repertoire of talks based on her experiences in television and one on her medical knowledge. By far the most popular with all kinds of audiences up and down the United Kingdom was one she titled: 'Fascinating people I have met.' It was an orgy of name-dropping – her co-stars Gilbert Harding, Barbara Kelly, David Nixon, Eamonn Andrews, Michael Denison and Robert Morley – and many others; from Baron, the photographer, to hairdresser Teasy-Weasy Raymond; Sir John Barbirolli to Henry Hall; Mai Zetterling to A. E. Matthews; Roger Bannister, the first four-minute miler, to Victor Barna, the great table-tennis champion; Danny Kaye to Boris Karloff. But not once did she allow her anecdotes to slide, as must have been so tempting, into unseemly gossip. The audiences loved the vicarious thrills of it all and she had to devise another talk, 'More fascinating people I have met', because she was always being asked back to regale the same groups a second time.

One of the items in her repertoire, 'The whys and wherefores of public speaking', was something of a waspish reaction to one of her own earlier engagements. Very new to the business and very nervous, she was forced to sit through a lunch with the chairman extolling the virtues of the previous week's guest who had talked about speaking in public and all about subconscious mannerisms and idiosyncrasies. By the time she was supposed to follow in the footsteps of this lady, she was so convinced that the audience was waiting to spot her deficiencies that she could hardly get to her feet with nerves.

By way of a riposte to the mauling she got from the weightier fashion writers, she delighted women's groups with her 'Coming to terms with fashion', in which she took great delight in pointing out some of the more ludicrous flights-of-fancy and stressed that it was more important to feel comfortable than to look like an immobile fashion-plate.

Even when she turned to medicine for her 'Why can't we live to 100?' talk, she worked in plenty of humour, though it was somewhat muted whenever she spoke to groups of professionals. Conscious that she really could not keep up-to-date with the many changes that were taking place, she was never very comfortable with her medical peers. They, however, were no less susceptible to her charm than were ordinary audiences, and she could have kept herself fully occupied on the doctors-and-nurses circuit if she had had the time.

Time, however, was always a problem for the energetic Lady Barnett. There were never enough hours in the day for all the things she wanted to do. The result was that with her television work, lecturing and all her public commitments, she ended up with a punishing schedule that kept her travelling the length and breadth of the country at a very hectic pace and always, of course, in the full glare of public attention wherever she went. It is hardly surprising, therefore, that she should sometimes become so desperate for a little privacy that her usual good manners gave way to common-or-garden selfishness, as was so clearly the case at the holiday hotel in Tenby. Why, though, should such a highly-intelligent woman extend herself to such extremes, spreading her energies thinly over such a wide range of activities? She certainly was not the vain, county-set lady anxiously trying to outdo her friends in the number of points she could score for good works. Too much of her personal effort was expended quietly and discreetly for that to be the case. Nor was money a particular lure. Although she loved having her own income, it was because it represented her independence rather than anything else. In fact, she and Sir Geoffrey were more than comfortably-off and neither of them needed to work. She always said that most of her earnings would go into a trust for young Alastair, and that is indeed what happened when she died, leaving an estate of more than £450,000.

A more likely cause for her seemingly relentless activity was that she was acutely aware that her television career, enjoyable as it very clearly was, did not give her any real sense of purpose. She was happy to find her excitement in front of the cameras but while she saw that entertaining the great British public was a perfectly valid occupation for some people, she – like her 'What's My Line?' co-panellist, Gilbert Harding – was also conscious that it was far from vital to society's deeper needs. In her weaker moments she admitted her regret at giving up general practice and with it the chance to make a worthwhile contribution to the local community. She must have felt particularly guilty about wasting her training, knowing that her place at medical school could have gone to someone else who would have devoted a lifetime to medicine.

Purposeful or not, however, Lady Barnett's appearances on television delighted the audiences and in 1956 she became the first person to win a double in the *News Chronicle*'s 'Television Top Ten' competition. She was named top woman's personality for her presentation of 'Look and Choose' and her interviewing on other afternoon programmes, and for her performance on 'What's My Line?' she was voted top *variety artist*, a category she could not have expected to win.

Her initial reaction? 'My husband will be as amazed as I am to hear that I have joined the variety profession,' she said, 'I don't do an act – I couldn't. I am myself and I enjoy myself on TV and hope some of it gets through to the viewers.' The newspaper described her popularity after only three years as 'phenomenal' and that is not an overstatement when you see her success in the context of the total winning-list: best regular programme, 'Sunday Night at the London Palladium'; best play, 'Jane Eyre'; best actor, Peter Cushing; best actress, Flora Robson; best musical artist, Eric Robinson; best commentator, Peter Scott; best outside broadcast, the F A Cup Final; and best commercial, Murraymints. Other names competing for the various prizes included Eamonn Andrews, Douglas Fairbanks Junior, Mai Zetterling and Peter Haigh. But, as the *News Chronicle* pointed out, Lady Barnett's success had not been earned easily: 'She has had to pay a price for it – in freedom! Last Saturday was the first in many weeks she had not turned the usual little speech into suitability for the opening of a bazaar. The day, spent riding and pottering about her big garden, was a rare oasis on an interminable round of television and personal appearances.'

It was, however, a price that Isobel seemed only too ready to pay in return for the continuing affection of the public, and the accolade of being named the best at what she had chosen to do as a new career seemed reasonable compensation for all the personal sacrifice.

There were, of course, moments when Lady Barnett was not quite so sure of her public esteem. Not long after the *News Chronicle* Awards, she and Sir Geoffrey were en route for a holiday on the French Riviera when there were reports that he had been killed in a car crash. As the press had checked out the story and found it to be untrue, they both assumed that the item would not be published. But for some unknown reason it did appear and by the time they arrived in Monte Carlo after an overnight stop in London, it was one of the talking points among the British holidaymakers there. They, of course, recognized Lady Barnett but not Sir Geoffrey and when they saw them walking arm-in-arm and dining together, there were some scandalized comments about Isobel being an 'odious creature' for enjoying herself with her husband newly dead. She in turn was horrified that 'her public' could so readily think badly of her and it was a long time before Sir Geoffrey could persuade her to see the funny side of the incident.

It was perhaps as well that Isobel never knew about Malcolm

Muggeridge's views of her role. Writing in his diary in March, 1957 (but which was not published until much later), he said: 'Caught train to Isle of Wight where I had to take part in "Any Questions?" radio programme. Sat in carriage with Lady Barnett, quite fascinating TV figure, also on programme. She seems to belong to TV screen. Decided that if seduceable at all, it could only be on television. In life, passionless, odourless, tasteless. Neatly dressed, with wonderful faculty for producing banalities with eagerness, even a sort of animation. Only tuned in to this world. No connection with any other. A Laputa girl.'

With some justification, Isobel's admirers would have seen that as unnecessarily cruel and they might have suggested that it was as much a commentary on Mr Muggeridge's professional waspishness as it was on her characteristics. It should certainly be seen in the context of some of his other diary notes in the 1950s. For example, he commented Ian Fleming was 'definitely a slob'; Hilaire Belloc was 'not a serene man . . . there seemed very little in him'; and Evelyn Waugh was a 'quite ludicrous figure'. He wrote off the beginning of a new genre of drama in describing John Osborne's *Look Back in Anger* as an 'inexecrable' play; and he found a Picasso exhibition nothing but 'excessively depressing'.

In assessing Lady Barnett, he had clearly cut through all the attendant adulation of her mass popularity, but his perception does not seem to have been acute enough for him to realize that he was seeing no more of her than did the television audiences. He was only observing in a less generous light the carefully self-sanitized public persona of a woman whose deeper thoughts and emotions were left safely at home in Leicestershire with her husband. She would have been no more ready to discuss her inner feelings with Malcolm Muggeridge than she would have been to parade naked through the streets of Leicester

If Mr Muggeridge was singularly unimpressed by her style of conversation, there were many other people more than ready to listen to anything she was prepared to say in public and, like him, she became a great favourite on 'Any Questions?' which was then chaired by Freddie Grisewood, one of Britain's most popular broadcasters. Indeed, that Isle of Wight occasion was the first of many on which they sat on the speakers' platform together. But what they seldom shared were their opinions. Malcolm's replies to the audience's topical questions almost always served to underline Isobel's innate conservatism.

On one programme, when the questioner asked to what extent the private lives of public figures should be allowed to affect their careers, Isobel was very positive: 'I think one of the great things in this country is that, by and large, we have been able to look up to the people who govern us and expect from them standards which perhaps in this too tolerant day and age we don't always apply to the man and woman in the street. I think, by and large, this has served us very well. There may have been occasions when somebody has been perhaps harshly judged, when a resignation perhaps was unmerited. But I think mostly our administration has been an honest, a graft-free one, and by and large, our public men on accepting public office have conformed to certain standards. I think this is something that we should go on expecting and something that we should not allow to sink in a tolerance which may be misplaced today.'

Malcolm favoured more tolerance, even if only out of realism: 'If you're going to say that men who commit adultery may not be ministers of the crown, or may not be headmasters of schools, or may not be this and may not be that, you are going to have very great difficulty in forming a government or finding anybody to preside over the various institutions of our society.'

Another questioner asked if ordinary people should ignore the *avant-garde* writers – this being the late 1950s – who were beginning to use much stronger language, to cling to the virtues of polite conversation. Malcolm assumed the man was obliquely referring to sex and replied that in his view, 'sex was enormously funny and therefore nice to talk about.' Isobel could not go along with such a remark, which she saw as much too flippant: 'Writers do seem to write about what they like, but an author will only stay in business if the public also likes what he writes. So presumably he's pleasing someone by writing these – to me – distressingly frank books. I think sex is a very important and a very splendid thing and I hate to see it reduced to four-letter words either in print or in conversation. So if we're going to talk about sex and all the things that interest us, let's do it at the level of higher, interesting conversation. And if you can only talk about it on the four-letter level, then neither write about it nor talk about it.'

Isobel's views might today be regarded as excessively straight-laced and even naïve, but then they were shared by many of the older generation at least. For her to be able to express them – even as genteely as she did on 'Any Questions?' – shows that she had come a long way from her prim, Presbyterian days when as a teenage university student she had walked out of the meeting of the Oxford Group. What neither she nor Malcolm Muggeridge could have been especially conscious of was that they were really rehearsing some of the arguments society at large was to go through as the drab and dreary Fifties finally gave way to what were to become known as the Swinging Sixties. It was not a particularly comfortable period to live through, but then, readjustments are never easy and Britain had to get used to the idea of a growth in prosperity. As the post-war rationing and restrictions fell away, there was a strong stirring of confidence, especially among the young people, and inevitably there was conflict as they refused to accept the old order. The generation gap widened and became a great gulf as Bill Haley, Elvis Presley and their various disciples invaded the front rooms and took over the Dansette gramophones everywhere.

Isobel Barnett's popularity at that stage was enough for her to bridge the gap and she could claim fans in all age groups. But she, too, was finding her changing situation less comfortable than she would have liked. She enjoyed all the fuss and attention but as the demands of television and public appearances grew, she found herself almost permanently hiding behind the carefully-contrived image and there was a great danger of her personal life shrivelling up altogether. She devoted every minute she had free to being with her husband and, when he was home from boarding-school, her son. Nothing was allowed to keep her away from Geoffrey and the White House for very long, but that meant there was even less time for all the old friends with whom she so desperately wanted to stay in touch. The scribbled notes gave way to neat, impersonal, typed letters which sometimes were not even signed by Isobel, but by the secretary trying to copy her signature. There are even one or two examples of notes and gift cards to friends being signed 'With affection – Isobel Barnett'. The telephone remained one of her lifelines but the calls became much briefer and less regular. Meetings for lunch or dinner became even rarer and, more often than not, they would be interrupted by one journalist or another. One of her friends from their days at Glasgow University, Dr Robert Shanks, recalls that at that stage Isobel seemed publicity-mad and was ready to give an interview on anything to anyone who asked.

Another old friend who had been out of touch with her for several years was astonished at the way the public image had developed in such contrast to the Isobel she had known. Rosemary Anderson had gone to school with Isobel at Laurel Bank in Glasgow and at the Mount in York and they had remained close enough friends for her to be godmother when Alastair was christened. She then joined the WRNS and served in various parts of the world and so missed the early days of Isobel's television career. When she came back to Britain, she met Isobel again at the Bath Club in London: 'I couldn't believe the change in her, especially in her voice and the kind of language she used. In her club with people like Joyce Grenfell and Osbert Sitwell around, she was "Darling" this and "Darling" that. I was very, very surprised, but when we were on our own she reverted to her old self and we had a lovely chat.'

Over the years, both Rosemary Anderson and Molly Cox noticed that Isobel was experiencing more and more difficulty in making the switch from public to private persona. 'She was such fun to be with that I greatly looked forward to my annual visits to the White House. I would sit back in the luxurious comfort of her beautiful home, very relaxed, thoroughly enjoying her highly-entertaining conversation ... but I was aware that she liked to be in charge of the conversation, and although very willing to discuss my problems, if her difficulties were ever touched on, she would shy away, make light of them or change the subject. This became more marked with each visit. Sometimes she would even physically move away so that further conversation was impossible.'

Rosemary Anderson was aware that however rare her visits, they were always limited to a single day, even when she travelled all the way from Glasgow: 'However hospitable she might have been and however enjoyable the meeting, if you stayed at the White House overnight, she had virtually said her goodbyes to you before you could pack your case in the morning! It had nothing to do with shortage of time; she only seemed able to cope with friends one day at a time.' And, according to another friend, only one friend at a time too. "Quite often there were several of us around at the same time and we could have had a reunion. But Isobel would never let more than one of us see her on any occasion. She always needed some sort of barrier to protect her from something."

If she was having some difficulties in her private life, Lady Barnett seemed to have no such problems with the adoring viewers. Her success on television has, of course, to be seen in the context of that still-developing medium struggling for recognition alongside the all-powerful radio. While she and her 'What's My Line?' colleagues were delighted to be watched by an audience of eight million, nearly double that number were regular listeners to radio, with some programmes – 'The Archers', for example – attracting nearer twenty million. Indeed, when the new commercial television service was introduced in the mid-fifties, it was the death of Grace Archer in the daily serial on the same day that stole all the newspaper headlines.

Lady Barnett was, therefore, fully justified in seeing it as yet another accolade when she was invited to join the journalist Nancy Spain and two young scriptwriters, Frank Muir and Denis Norden, in a brilliant, new radio programme called 'My Word'. The show was devised by Tony Shryane and Edward J. Mason who, as producer and co-writer respectively, had had a very important role in the amazing success of 'The Archers', and it was chaired by the popular cricket commentator, John Arlott. The idea was simply to play with words and Lady Barnett teamed up with Frank Muir to show their skill in the use of the English language. She was astonished by the sharp-wittedness of the other three panellists – all, of course, professional word-smiths – and quickly realized she was out of her depth.

Intelligent as she was, she knew that she did not have a particularly creative or original mind and that her talent was in reacting to the stimulus of other people. 'My Word' called for originality from all the participants and Lady Barnett survived only six programmes. 'She was a very professional lady,' recalls Tony Shryane, 'and she knew the programme simply wasn't her cup of tea. She left by mutual agreement and without the slightest bit of ill-feeling on either side.'

Lady Barnett was, of course, disappointed at her failure to grasp another opportunity to broadcast, but, as it was a new programme, there had not been a great deal of publicity and she was soon able to shrug it off without too much fuss. In any case, she was still much too busy to let it prey on her mind and there was barely a hiccup in her routine of public appearances.

The Barnetts at home in the early 1960s.

One of many public appearances, with Sir Geoffrey in the background.

Dear Best—,

Words cannot ever tell you of my gratitude for all that you have done to ease my path during the past sad weeks.

I would like you to have this little thing to remember him b——. He was so fond of you.

Thank you for giving so much warmth and loving kindness when I needed it most.

Affectionately,

Isobel B——arnett.

During a visit to a bazaar in 1978, Lady Barnett allowed a graphologist to study a sample of her handwriting and admitted that his assessment was very accurate. His report read: 'A highly individual worker with ideas of her own. Tense, taut, she does everything with great intensity and much high pressure. She has good artistic and dramatic sense and a keen sense of presentation.

'Precise, accurate and single-minded, she tends to be decisive and see one point of view. Somewhat rigid and fixed but has high standards and is a stickler for precision.

'She knows exactly what she wants and is not usually given to compromise once she has come to a conclusion. Accustomed to having her own way by strength of personality and conviction rather than aggression.

'Health seems good but tense and somewhat brittle. Temper usually good. Sharp, decisive, nervous anger when roused. It does not last but I am sure it takes a great deal out of her.

'A somewhat temperamental, emotional nature, she has wide human sympathies but has no illusions and does not suffer fools gladly.

'I think she finds herself living under considerable strain and the glare of publicity does not help or make life any easier.'

Isobel adjudicates a
competition.

The White House.

Isobel at home, by her newly-installed swimming pool. (*Keystone Press*).

In the late 1970s, relaxing among the flowers. (*Keystone Press*)

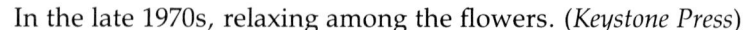

CHAPTER 11

As she faced the start of a new decade, Lady Barnett was able to look ahead and see only continuing success. After seven years, she was so well established that few people would have been able to remember what television was like without her. Her name had become synonymous with 'What's my Line?' and there were no signs of any diminution in her phenomenal popularity. Her secretary was handling so many appeals for personal appearances that she could have booked her up for nearly five years ahead and there simply were not enough hours in the day for all the things other people wanted her to do.

One minor problem was that she found it very difficult to say 'no' to people and no matter how hard she tried to channel everything through her secretary, there were always some who managed to waylay her personally. In the end, because of the sheer weight of invitations, she was forced to impose a sliding scale of fees, according to whether or not she wanted or was able to attend any function. For those engagements she did not want, she would demand an enormous fee, knowing full well that that would act as a deterrent or that if it did not she would at least be well paid for her trouble. For her friends and for her favourite charities, she would go to any lengths and not charge a penny.

She thought nothing of driving from her home in Leicestershire to Crawley in Sussex to talk to a group of church women, just because she had been asked to by Molly Cox, whose husband was then the local curate. Nor did she hesitate when the invitation was from any group around her own village. Jack Meadows, a retired journalist and parish councillor, worked for charity with Lady Barnett for many years: 'Few people realize just how much she did around here. She was a very feeling woman and was always ready to help anyone who needed it without waiting to be asked.'

She was also happy to use her influence in a good cause and

whenever appeals for help reached her, she would persuade one of the voluntary organizations to handle it if it was something beyond her own competence. For example, one pensioner wrote saying she could not afford a roll of wire-netting to put around her garden so that her dog – which had already almost been run over – could be kept out of harm's way. Lady Barnett contracted the WVS near the old lady's home and within days they had put up a fence. But not only that, they also discovered that she produced very beautiful tapestry and they were able to market it for her and supplement her meagre income.

Molly Cox remembers another occasion when Lady Barnett responded to a personal appeal in a particularly practical as well as thoughtful way. Molly, the great letter-writer, had kept in touch with many of her other schoolfriends, and she learned from Rosemary Anderson that one of the Mount's old girls had got into serious difficulties and was desperately in need of help. Her parents had divorced when she was very young and when her own marriage broke up, she suffered a serious nervous breakdown. By the time Rosemary got to know about it, the girl had been in a mental hospital for several years and her condition was so improved that she was ready to be released. The authorities, however, were very reluctant to let her go without somebody to effectively sponsor her to a new start. Rosemary wrote to many old Mount girls: 'We thought if we could raise enough money between us, I could act as that sponsor. Everyone I contacted was very kind and I did collect quite a lot of cash. But Isobel was so much more thoughtful than the rest of us. She did not simply sit down and sign a cheque as I had hoped she might. She had worked out the problem in her own mind and assessed that the girl's morale would be very low and that money alone wasn't the answer. She said that in such cases it was just as important to feed the ego as to do anything else; so she sent a great parcel of lovely clothes which, she said, would help to get her back on her feet that much more quickly than if she was left with decisions about something as basic as what to wear when she got up in the morning. That kind of constructive thoughtfulness was typical of Isobel – and, of course, she was right!'

Lady Barnett had the knack of being right more often than not and her comprehensive cleverness sometimes irked her friends, not because she ever sought to belittle anyone, but simply because it served to underline their own imperfections. For her fans, however, it was yet another of her endearing qualities and for the journalists who seemed to dog her every footstep, it made her one of the most quotable personalities in the land.

Despite her privileged upbringing and her own right-wing politics, she nearly always managed to voice the feelings of ordinary people. She was, for example, one of the first publicly to express her concern about the growing influence of television. It was, she said, like a 'wild and savage beast' – harmless if properly controlled but very dangerous if not constantly supervised. It should not, therefore, be allowed to dominate the home but should be seen as making a worthwhile contribution to family entertainment and education.

Hire purchase was another of the worrying issues of the day, and when she was asked about it on radio's 'Any Questions?' she was sensibly cautious about the live-now-pay-later syndrome: 'I think what is terrifying today is the hard sell that is practised – perhaps not so much in the country districts – but in the suburbs of big cities. You get these terrifying salesmen who come round and pressurise a woman into signing forms which, quite often, she hasn't even read properly. Then she's let in for a burden of debt which she doesn't get rid of for the next ten years – always providing that all goes well with the family. But if sickness or unemployment comes along, then the family is in a really terrible mess. So let's have hire purchase in proper proportion and then I think it can go hand in hand with thrift.'

Of course, not all the questions were serious. At a programme in Cornwall, the team members were asked what gift they would bestow on a newborn child and in her answer, Isobel revealed something of her own ambition: 'I think I would give the gift of joyfulness, of being able to take on anything and really find pleasure in it. There are people who have this gift. They are wonderful to be with, and I think that not only are they happy – they spread happiness around them, too. The most terrible things they see as a joke. They are able to turn them into something gay and funny, and that would be the gift I'd like to give my godchild.'

Those who choose to court mass popularity – whether they be television personalities or politicians – are, of course, riding dangerously on the back of the tiger, and it was perhaps the excitement of risk-taking that held most appeal for Lady Barnett. Like an inveterate gambler, she used her consummate skill in playing the game, testing her nerve as she tried to keep her finger on the public pulse and, all the time, keeping her own self closely guarded. By getting it right so often, she was able to maintain her inevitably-precarious position at the top with remarkable confidence.

We now know, of course, what happened in 1980 when she failed to read the likely reaction of just twelve members of her public at her trial; but then, in 1960, the only apparent cloud on her horizon was a growing anxiety about her husband's health. Sie Geoffrey's condition had never been very strong since the illness which, five years earlier, had forced him to give up his political ambition. When he started complaining about excruciating pains in his chest which spread to his arms and neck, it was clear he was suffering from arteriosclerosis – the early stages of hardening of the arteries – and with her medical knowledge, Isobel was only too well aware of the consequential danger of thrombosis or a stroke if he did not take life very much easier.

It was not until some years later that medical research showed the condition to be a disease likely to result from the stresses and strains of modern living. In 1960, it was thought to be simply the inevitable consequence of the natural ageing process, and although he was only fifty-seven, Sir Geoffrey was persuaded to retire early – at least from the rigours of the day-to-day running of his busy solicitor's practice. He insisted on carrying on with his other business interests which were, in any case, less arduous.

Sir Geoffrey's ill-health also had the effect of making the sixteen-year age gap between him and Isobel look even wider. At forty-two – and despite her chain-smoking – she was in her prime and still full of boundless energy, while he was beginning to stoop and suffered from sluggishness. But there was no question of them drifting apart. Isobel was still very dependent on Sir Geoffrey. He had done a great deal to groom her as a gracious lady and his quiet authority had saved her from her own wilder excesses. In fact, she had confessed to Molly Cox that the most important reason for her marrying Geoffrey was that she simply knew he was the only man she had ever met who would have been strong enough to keep her under control. It is an explanation that makes sense, because, as many of their friends observed, the two did not have too many things in common. He was a quiet, shy man whose natural reserve gave him a diffident air which belied his actual toughness; she was bouncy and bright, really at her happiest in a crowd where she was the centre of attention. He had a small appetite and only a passing interest in food; she was a *bon viveur* with a passion for food and wine. He could not be bothered with gardening; she loved to plant bulbs and kept hundreds of plants in the house. Despite their different natures, they were a very loving couple and it was Sir Geoffrey's great personal strengths that allowed Isobel the enormous freedom she had to exploit the opportunities arising from her television career. A lesser man would not have been so ready to tolerate her constant absences.

Once again, however, the admiring public were given no clue as to Lady Barnett's private anxieties. The only outward signs were her determined efforts to spend a little more time with Geoffrey at home, which meant hours spent on draughty railway stations waiting for last trains, or hectic car drives in the small hours.

By this time, she was the longest-serving member of the 'What's My Line?' panel and her reward was to be named again in the annual showbusiness polls – this time as Television Personality of the Year – and to win the title 'Indestructible' from the readers of the *Daily Mail*. 'Lady Barnett ... is one of the Indestructibles of our time,' wrote columnist Eve Perrick. 'The gracious Isobel is in the groove. If not quite "with it" hipwise, she is certainly still with us.' And to prove just how much she was with us, the paper listed her activities over a twelve day period:

WEDNESDAY: In London for meeting of National Film Committee.

THURSDAY: In Birmingham opening the sampling kitchen of a custard company. On to Bristol for some ceremonial in connection with a home for the disabled and then a recording of an appeal at the local BBC studios.

FRIDAY: In Cornwall for an 'Any Questions?' broadcast.

SATURDAY: At home.

SUNDAY: In London for the first show of the 'What's My Line?' eleventh season [her ninth, going on tenth year at the game].

MONDAY: In Leicester taking the chair at the National Hospital Services Annual meeting.

TUESDAY: Luncheon – 'What do we do for the youth of Leicester?'

WEDNESDAY: 'Resting' with only a house-guest to entertain.

THURSDAY: Shipley, Yorkshire, for a paid lecture [thirty-five guineas less fifteen per cent, of which her sponsor, Maurice Winnick, gets half agents' fees].

FRIDAY: Dundee – lecture.

SATURDAY: Back home for the wedding of her house-keeper's daughter, an engagement which gives Lady Barnett particular pleasure because the staircase in her Georgian house is 'just perfect for a bride to come down.'

SUNDAY: At home with just the film version of 'What's My Line?' to watch for points.

That was, in fact, a fairly quiet spell for Lady Barnett – she did not often get two consecutive Saturdays at home – but even so it still adds up to about two thousand miles of travelling. Said Eve Perrick: 'Now that's quite a programme for anyone, even an athletic type with expert medical knowledge, to undertake – and like it. Lady Barnett likes it. She says: "I'm a dreary woman doing dreary things," but she says it with no conviction whatever. Because, as she knows and I know you know, that just isn't true. Lady B is not a dreary woman. She has proved herself quick off the mark, on the uptake, and in her reflexes on all occasions.'

Lady Barnett was usually very coy about how much money she earned, but on this occasion, she confessed to earning about £6,000 a year and that she liked the money: 'No one ever has enough money of her own. This way I am independent enough to be extravagant about clothes when I feel like it. I've always enjoyed clothes and now I do have the occasions to wear them. Before all this, when I was living the life of a countrywoman, as long as I had a bazaar hat and a reasonable suit, I never had a good excuse to indulge.'

Of her success, Lady Barnett had no secrets to offer: 'I can't understand why I've been able to go on for so long as it is. I'm not an actress – I can't learn a line of script. I don't have any original thoughts or brilliant ideas for doing something new. So I'm more than happy, even grateful, to be able to continue guessing people's occupations, lecturing to women's clubs, opening stores, compèring fashion shows – anything or any place where I can meet people. If it all came to a sudden stop I should miss it, of course, but it wouldn't surprise me in the least.'

This last remark to Eve Perrick was without doubt the first step in Lady Barnett's self-preparation for the inevitable. Although she had eight astonishingly-successful years behind her, she did not altogether share the *Daily Mail* readers' wide-eyed optimism. She knew only too well that no one was 'indestructible' in the ephemeral world of television and that, therefore, her bubble was bound to burst sooner or later. Since that improbable 'What's My Line?' debut in 1953, she had somehow beaten the odds and her personal popularity had kept pace with the remarkable advance of television itself from the Cinderella days when it struggled in the shadow of radio to its emergence as one

112

of the most potent influences on the British way of life. Nevertheless, her experience of seeing so many other personalities come and go during that time had bred caution. She sensed that her own bandwagon's breakneck speed had been already checked and was quietly steeling herself against the day when it might finally come to a halt and it was her turn to fade away.

It was not a happy thought and, as she did so often, Lady Barnett quickly consigned it to the deeper recesses of her mind, where it was safe from the sympathy of friends. But it was always there and, perhaps conscious of it, she seemed more than ever to live for the day. Without noticeably curtailing her punishing schedule of public appearances, she devoted more and more energy to her family life. She went swimming and riding with Alastair whenever he was home from the agricultural training college where he was now studying farm management. She played golf and bridge with Sir Geoffrey whenever he could be persuaded to relax and take time off from his remaining business interests. And she still found time to arrange a series of glittering parties at the White House.

The cooking and most of the preparation for all the entertaining was the responsibility of Mrs Sybil Lines, who worked as housekeeper to Lady Barnett for more than thirty years: 'Those were really happy times. We had garden parties, lunches, cocktail parties, dinners, suppers, and there were nearly always several well known names on the guest-list – celebrities from television, the theatre and even from films. It was lovely. Sir Geoffrey and Lady Barnett were wonderful hosts and everyone seemed to enjoy themselves so much. The house was always full of laughter.'

The Barnetts were themselves guests at a very special cocktail party in 1962 – at Buckingham Palace. For the dedicated name-dropper it was a dream come true as the Queen and Prince Philip hosted an informal gathering of about fifty people. The 'scalps' Lady Barnett collected that evening included John Mills, the actor (now Sir John Mills), Dai Rees, the golfer, George Harriman, managing director of the British Motor Corporation (now BL Cars Ltd), dramatist Christopher Fry and a bevy of MPs that included Mrs Margaret Thatcher, then a very junior minister in the Macmillan Government.

It would, under almost any circumstances, have been an enjoyable and fascinating experience – in fact, as it turned out, it was the forerunner of many similar informal gatherings – but it was made even more memorable for Lady Barnett when she learned to her absolute delight that Sunday nights at the Palace were never complete without 'What's My Line?' on television. It was a piece of information she simply could not resist dropping into her conversation and the first opportunity came when she sat at the same table as Arthur Helliwell, top columnist of the Sunday newspaper, *The People*, at a function at the Savoy Hotel. Like the good journalist he was, he snapped it up and was more than happy to relay the news of the Royal Patronage to his millions of readers, most of whom, he knew, were also likely to be fans of Lady Barnett.

It was at the same table that she let slip a clue that she was still bottling up her natural feelings. Outwardly so cool and calm, she told Arthur Helliwell that she was 'dying to let her hair down and become a roaring, raging female Gilbert Harding.' And, as he put it: 'Behind that ice-cool, gently-smiling façade that ten million viewers know so well, there is a fire-breathing tigress struggling to escape.' What he did not know was that Isobel had learned to control the tigress – her sharp tongue and devastating disdain – away back in her school days and what she was saying now provided more evidence that her overriding concern had always been what other people might think of her, to the extent that she had spent more than half her lifetime trying to stifle her natural temperament. Strong as her instincts were to survive so long under such circumstances, her self-control was even stronger. As later events were to show, too much control can be dangerous and it would perhaps have been better for her if she had given vent to her feelings rather than holding them in check.

In Isobel's own whimsical estimation, such a release might also have led to a more entertaining 'What's My Line?' She told Arthur Helliwell: 'If only I had the moral courage, I would let go. Time after time when we get a particularly evasive or infuriating contestant, I sit there longing to blow my top in one of dear Gilbert's typical outbursts. I'd give anything to be able to explode. The show really needs the fireworks we got from Gilbert.' (When Gilbert Harding had died two years earlier, in 1960, the obituary in *The Times* said that 'the lights seemed to have dimmed' since he no longer appeared on the programme.)

There is no doubt that the show had lost much of its sparkle and Arthur Helliwell wondered: 'How has Lady Barnett survived the maddeningly monotonous trivialities for so long with no visible scars? She has a wealthy husband and therefore she doesn't *have* to do it for a living. But it seems she really enjoys it. "It's fun and I'm never bored with the show," she insists. She enjoys even more, I suspect, the recognition that television fame has brought.'

Mr Helliwell's suspicion was well founded. Of course she enjoyed her popularity: who would not get enormous pleasure from being loved by so many people? He was also quite right in saying that she showed no *visible* scars after her long stint on the programme. No one at that time would have had any real reason to believe anything other than that Lady Barnett was riding comfortably on the tiger's back. It is only in retrospect that there is a suspicion she was beginning to run up some very heavy emotional bills which she was not able to pay in 1980.

If Lady Barnett was not showing scars, the programme itself was beginning to show its age. Twelve years is a very long time in television and what had been a bright, innovative show to the viewers in 1951 was looking a lot less fashionable in the early 1960s. When the inevitable happened and – in August 1963 – the BBC decided to drop 'What's My Line?' from the schedules, no one was really surprised. While it had remained virtually unchanged, Britain was a very different place. Post-war gloom had given way to a new mood of optimism – with television, many will say, having played quite an important role in the general transformation. In 1963 we were also assaulted by the news as never before. It was the year President Kennedy was shot in Dallas; Pope John XXIII died; and there were earthquakes in Skopje in Yugoslavia. In Britain there was the Profumo Affair; the Great Train Robbery; Dr Beeching took his axe to the railways; there were the worst unemployment figures for sixteen years (878,356); Hugh Gaitskell died and Harold Wilson became leader of the Labour Party; Harold Macmillan resigned and, after renouncing his title, Sir Alec Douglas-Home became Prime Minister. In such circumstances, it is hardly surprising that the fading from the screen of 'What's My Line?' did not exactly cause a revolution.

CHAPTER 12

*P*redictable or not, and whatever it might have meant to anyone else, the end of 'What's My Line?' must have felt a bit like the end of the world to Lady Barnett. It had first transformed her life, taking her from the genteel Shires and setting her on the fairytale path to national stardom. Then it had dominated her every waking moment for ten years. It had given her an unexpected *entrée* to the glamourous world of showbusiness, access to half the homes in Britain, and it provided some of the adrenalin-stirring excitement for which she had craved. However much she might have tried to prepare herself for the moment, it must still have been an awful shock when the red studio warning light went out for the last time.

On the surface, of course, there was not a flicker of concern. Her public attitude was that all good things must come to an end and, in any case, she had had more than a good run for her money. 'It's all been a delightful frolic,' she said. 'I never at any time felt it was a career.' In an interview in her local paper, the *Leicester Mercury*, she gave the impression that it was almost a blessing in disguise because it meant she would have more time for her friends and her golf and her bridge.

She was, however, genuinely grateful for the experience and said so: 'In a childish kind of way, I really enjoyed the game ... meeting interesting and famous people.' And she was mindful that she had not achieved her success single-handed: 'My cup of gratitude ought to be a challenge cup – a teacup would not be large enough to include the producers who have supported me morally and physically, when necessary; the other performers who have exuded friendly co-operation from every pore; and everyone – from the cameraman to the stage-doorkeeper at the Television Theatre – who have cheered me on my erratic way.'

It was a genuine, if effusive, note of gratitude but it surprisingly overlooked the people who had been most important to her success and who had cheered her on her way most enthusiastically – the audience. It was a sad omission because it was the ordinary viewers who had so readily taken her to their hearts and who – despite her title and her obvious elevated social status – made her *their* representative on the new medium of television. Whether it was because of the title or because, as a panellist, she was always set against the Establishment's representative – chairman Eamonn Andrews – Lady Barnett was never seen as just another professional. Her admirers were more than ready to listen to her views or take her advice in a way that would be inconceivable with any of today's stars. But if she forgot to say thanks on this occasion, it was the first time she had let them down in any way. They had chosen their champion well and her basic commonsense approach – plus an unerring ability to judge the public mood – allowed her to be the voice of what the Americans call the Silent Majority.

When 'What's My Line?' came off, Lady Barnett suffered absolutely no loss in public esteem. She was as much in demand for lectures and after-dinner speeches as ever before and she continued making occasional appearances on other television programmes and, more regularly, taking part in 'Any Questions?', 'Twenty Questions', 'Many a Slip', 'Petticoat Line' and several others of the great radio favourites.

There was only the odd tell-tale sign to suggest that she might be somewhat less sanguine than she pretended to be about the loss of her weekly, peak-hour platform. Since the beginning of the year, she had been keeping a New Year's resolution to cut down on cigarettes – which were then seen as almost *de rigueur* for the sophisticated woman – but when the programme ended her resolve weakened and she was soon back to her old habit of smoking more than sixty a day. It should be said, of course, that she was also worrying about Sir Geoffrey's health and suffering some anxiety about the choice of career for Alastair. Her old university friend, Dr Robert Shanks, however, has no doubts about what bothered her most: 'She was very upset when the programme was taken off because she so valued her distinguished acquaintances and she must have seen in it the danger to her favourite pastime of name-dropping! More importantly, of course, she saw in the inevitable loss of publicity – and at that stage she was publicity-mad – a likely fall-off in bookings for all her other things like personal appearances and lectures.'

Lady Barnett did admit that she was apprehensive about that, not because she needed the money but because she had what some of her friends regarded as a near-obsessional concern about her son's future. Sadly it was a subject she could not properly discuss with Sir Geoffrey because it was the poor state of his general health that gave rise to her anxiety in the first place. As she saw the signs of premature aging in him, she undoubtedly felt that she would have to be responsible for providing financial security for young Alastair, and it was a responsibility that weighed heavily on her slim shoulders. She had seen what had happened when her own father had died – a drastic drop in the family income and her enforced departure from the Mount – and she was desperately anxious that Alastair should not be affected in the same way.

'Unless you knew Isobel exceptionally well, you would never have guessed she had any real cares in the world,' says Dr Shanks. 'She always put on such a brave face.' And Molly Cox adds: 'Even as a schoolgirl she never cried. Only in her letters did she admit difficulties. Only once did I ever see Isobel break down. It was a few months after Geoffrey's death. We had met at her club. She was returning to "Many A Slip" and she'd asked me to accompany her. While talking quite easily about Geoffrey, something made her lose control. Immediately she said, "Talk to me about Jono" – my youngest son. I did, just stroking her arm to show I understood and in minutes she had completely regained her composure. No one saw a single tear throughout her traumatic trial in 1980.

Not long after 'What's My Line?' finished, Lady Barnett received an extraordinary invitation which, if it did not replace the excitement of television, did at least demand a great deal of her time and gave her some sense of purpose. She was asked to join the committee set up by the government to enquire into factory-farming methods. The invitation was surprising partly because it came from the Labour Government – Harold Wilson was Prime Minister and Fred Peart (now Lord Peart) was Minister of Agriculture – but more so because it was a technical committee under the chairmanship of Professor F. W. Rogers Brambell. Not only was she the only woman on the committee, she was also the only lay member. It is a mark of the considerable regard in which she was held that no one demurred from the assumption that she was more than capable of making a worthwhile contribution to the debate.

For more than a year, alongside eight of the country's leading experts on animal husbandry, veterinary care, animal behaviour and agriculture, Lady Barnett listened to the complex arguments about the various methods of intensive-farming and heard evidence from dozens of interested parties. The committee travelled all over Britain – from East Anglia to Ulster and from Sussex to the north of Scotland – and also went to see what was happening in Denmark and the Netherlands.

Factory-farming was one of the most controversial issues of the day, arousing as it did the passions of every animal welfare group in the land, and Lady Barnett took the long deliberations very seriously indeed. But away from the committee she allowed people to think she was terribly blasé about it all by regaling her friends and acquaintances with hilarious stories about battery-hens and broilers, sweat-houses and piglet tail-biting.

It is never possible with government enquiries to determine the influence of individuals, but when the Brambell Committee finally reported, it used the sort of straight-forward language one would expect from Lady Barnett and its findings had strong roots in commonsense and majority public opinion: 'We accept that although pain, suffering and stress are certainly not identical in animals and man, there are sound reasons for believing they are substantial in domestic animals and there is no reason for disregarding them. It is claimed that suffering of any kind is reflected by a corresponding fall in productivity. The argument is that in the absence of any scientific method of evaluating whether an animal is suffering, its continued productivity can be taken as decisive evidence that it is not. That is an oversimplified and incomplete view and we reject it.'

The committee then went on to make a series of recommendations, including a new law, to ensure proper protection for farm animals. The animal welfare lobby was delighted but the farmers were not. They said the suggestions would add millions of pounds to their costs and would therefore put up food prices. The report then lay on a Whitehall shelf for about three years until, in 1968, a voluntary code of practice was issued.

For her part, Lady Barnett was content that she had done her best to try to get things changed. With all her usual energy and determination, she had made sure that her voice – which she saw as speaking on behalf of the ordinary man in the street – had been heard loudly and clearly on the issue and she felt quite confident that, sooner or later, the recommended code of practice would be taken up and followed by Britain's farmers. At least she saw no good reason to raise any personal objection when Alastair left agricultural training college and went to help manage a deep-litter poultry farm.

She also felt, with justification, that her contribution to the debate was an important pointer to the increasing role that women could play in public life. At a conference in Nottingham, she said: 'There is still a lot of prejudice against women in public life, but gradually more and more people are realising just what an important job we can do.' Then, without realizing it, she set herself up as an example: 'There's ample scope in local government work and in the local magistrates' courts as well as helping the needy and infirm. I believe there is specially room for women in juvenile courts, for we are in a much better position to understand young offenders of the law than men, for it is us who are with the children most of the time.' But by way of proof that feminism was still a thing of the future, she cautioned: 'When a woman begins married life, it is, of course, her main duty to look after her home and her husband and family. However by the time she had reached the age of thirty, she will, in most cases, have no children of a young and tender age, and will have more time to devote to other interests – and those interests should include public work.'

Few women would have been able to match Lady Barnett's boundless energy and organizational skill that allowed her to pack more into a week than many managed in a lifetime. During her years on 'What's My Line?' she had somehow come to terms with the relentless tyranny of the week-in-week-out commitment and still found time for so many other things. When the programme finished, the Brambell Committee came along and dropped very neatly into the gap. But when the committee's deliberations were concluded, she once more had time on her hands to ponder the future. Despite her fears, the end of 'What's My Line?' had not led to any loss of interest in her as a guest speaker and her diary was still well filled with engagements. She did not, therefore, have to worry much about finding things to do, but she was apprehensive about no longer having a central purpose because, whatever anyone else might have thought, her television work had become very important in her life.

There was no easy solution to her problem. Her medical qualifications were no longer of any real value because she had been out of general practice for so long and was therefore out of touch with the considerable developments there had been in medicine. She certainly could not go back to being a doctor. Nor, as she would have been the first to admit, was she well qualified to do much else professionally. Her television experience was only of value *in* television. Luckily she had no real ambition in life, except to be good at whatever was on the cards at any one time and one of her regular sayings was: 'If anything comes along, it comes along!'

As we now know, nothing else ever did come along to rekindle her excitement, but then she was quite philosophical and, instead of waiting in hope, she pressed on with other projects, including one in the City. When her mother died in 1954, she had inherited a small portfolio of investments and over the years she had, with Sir Geoffrey's advice and encouragement, built it up into a fascinating and profitable sideline. Typically, she was self-deprecating about her success: 'I'm a most unadventurous investor ... not one of those who are going to set the Thames on fire.' A friend in the City was more generous: 'She's an extremely intelligent woman with a very good grasp of investment matters.' Whether or not that was true or because there was no real enthusiasm for putting a torch to the Thames anyway, Lady Barnett was invited to be one of the first directors of a unit trust. Casting her modesty aside, she joined the Family Savings Trust, which was set up to specialize in consumer shares and was shrewdly aimed particularly at women investors, and promptly became a member of the prestigious Institute of Directors. If her new 'line' could not replace the lost excitement, at least it could add substance to her career.

With fractionally more time on her hands than for many years, Lady Barnett was able to devote more attention to maintaining contact with her old friends. Rosemary Anderson and Robert Shanks in Scotland found her telephone calls becoming a little more frequent, more conversational and much more entertaining: 'She stopped apologizing for being in a hurry and just chatted about everything under the sun.' Molly Cox noticed that the secretary-typed letters had once more given way to personally-written notes, although they still bore evidence of the tempo of her lifestyle: 'excuse hurried scrawl', 'must dash', 'life is frantic'. But after a faltering start to their renewed correspondence, Isobel was soon writing with all her old gusto and style:

You must think I am 'The End'. Way back in August you send me a book and from me no acknowledgement! There is however an explanation. The parcel arrived while we were in Italy, and the house was full of workmen tearing up the kitchen floor and painting the back part of the house. As everything was dust and chaos my dotty couple put your parcel and two others in the box room and forgot about them. I sacked them soon after we got home, and it was only yesterday that when I went in to sort out Christmas decorations, I discovered three parcels. Yours is bad enough but the others are frightful. They were from Harrods and I had played Cain about their non-arrival and the goods had been replaced. Now I shall have to write a *mea culpa* letter to them.

The book mentioned in the letter was a thank you gift from Molly for the hospitality she and her family had received on their first visit to the White House. It was an occasion that Isobel enjoyed as much as the Cox family and her next letter made that plain:

Shall I be seeing you this year en route for the North? Do let me know if it is on the cards. Love to see you all again. We are just recovering from the church garden fête. 1000 people milling round. Where they all come from I know not. But we raised the wonderful total of £700 and as it was dry the garden didn't suffer. But oh how we weeded, hoed and dug in preparation. I have collected a small thrush as a constant gardening companion. It never leaves me and as I hoe it picks up all the delectable grubs and worms. It obviously thinks I'm a better meal ticket than mother!

Lady Barnett's most regular broadcasting at the time was as team-mate of Eleanor Summerfield against David Nixon and Richard Murdoch on radio's 'Many A Slip'. It was a supposedly light-hearted contest but it worked better for the listeners when the panellists took it seriously – which they did, as was obvious from another letter:

I go to London tomorrow for the last recording. Eleanor and I are in the happy position of being two up and two to go so we can't lose. We were 'done' by The Critics on radio last Sunday and were all too frightened to listen so Charles Maxwell played us the recording last week. In fact they were very kind, but referred to poor Eleanor as a well known radio and TV personality. After RADA and all her years on the stage that was a little hard.

Between letters, Lady Barnett also found time to produce two more books. The first was *Exploring London*, a Shell Junior Guide which was illustrated by the cartoonist, Ronald Searle. The second, more individual effort, was *Lady Barnett's Cookbook*, intended to make life easier for the hostess who had to do her own cooking: 'There are three kinds of hostess cooks: the lucky ones who press their guests into service to cut bread and butter, watch the sprouts and stir the sauce. The clever ones who can cook in chafing-dishes before your very eyes, without getting spotted with hot fat and wiping their hands on their best dresses. Then the others, poor dears, of whom I am one, who like to have everything ready and waiting so that they can relax and enjoy their guests from the moment they arrive instead of doing a series of ten-second sprints between kitchen and sitting-room throughout the meal.'

Not surprisingly, she therefore concentrated on dishes that could be made in advance of the guests arriving, or which could be half-prepared and then needed only the minimum of last-minute fiddling. Apart from having the invaluable services of her housekeeper, Mrs Lines, Lady Barnett had another advantage over the average woman – a rather special kitchen: 'My present kitchen is the size of the average London flat and it has numerous commodious offshoots. A scullery, an enormous back kitchen, a laundry and a larder built for the good old days, with fly-proof cupboards, stone slabs, and hooks hanging from the ceiling for hams, venison and pheasants.' The kitchen, she said, was the most important room in the house: 'It isn't cooking that gets you down, it's drudgery. So the kitchen *must* be labour-saving.' As usual, despite her differing personal circumstances, her advice was sensible and apt.

As a break from her literary endeavours, Lady Barnett was able to indulge another favourite pastime. Travelling had always been one of her greatest pleasures, and after trips to Italy and France, she jumped at the chance to accompany Sir Geoffrey when he went to America on business. His group of companies' interests included mining-equipment and the visit was to the coalfields of West Virginia where, to her surprise, her celebrity status was well-known, resulting in VIP treatment wherever they went. Then, on her return with Sir Geoffrey to England, she found an invitation to take part in a new television quiz. With visions of another 'What's My Line?' in the offing, she immediately accepted, without asking for details. As she told Molly Cox, she later got quite a surprise:

At the moment I am involved in an extraordinary TV set up. The BBC asked me to do a quiz in Leicester. That was all I knew, and as Alastair was home he drove me in to park the car and lend Mum his moral support. I found to my astonishment that it was a sporting quiz and I was playing for Leicester City against Dundee United. Alastair was hysterical. As he said, 'Well I've seen everything. I never thought to cheer on my Mother playing for the City and to hear little boys shouting up the City, well played Barnett.' After we had defeated Dundee I found to my dismay that it is a knock out contest between 16 clubs, and I now have to play away and may land up at Wembley!

To her relief, Leicester did not make it to the final and 'Quizball,' as the programme was called, proved not to be a new launch pad for her. But as was clear from her letters, she was feeling much more relaxed about her son's future. He had set his foot on the first rung of the ladder in his new career and was working so hard he had missed the Christmas break at home:

He was in sole charge of 20,000 chickens and five chicken girls. He telephoned in the middle of dinner sounding quite unbelievably merry. He informed me he was drinking something very refreshing called Planters' Punch. Never met it before but just the job for a party. As he is well nigh a teetotaller except for an occasional glass of sherry or champagne – no wonder he was merry with all that refreshing rum inside him! I feel for his 20,000 chickens this morning.

With Alastair looking reasonably settled in his new career and Sir Geoffrey's health not getting any worse, Lady Barnett was able to accept an invitation that underlined her continuing popularity – to be guest speaker at an international congress on advertising in Canada. Her comments were reported on both sides of the Atlantic: 'I cannot believe, although I should like to, that I will grow a little lovelier each day because I use a certain soap. But I will buy a soap because you tell me that it is pure, mild, superfatted, kind to the skin, lathers magnificently, keeps BO at bay, leaves me bathed in a fragrant aroma. I may even buy the soap of film stars, feeling that even though I may not have as much money, as many swimming pools, or as many husbands as they do, we at least have a soap in common. But I will not buy something in which I cannot believe. My beauty, or lack of it, is there and no soap is going to alter it.'

The Canadian trip was just before her forty-ninth birthday and when she came back to Britain, one of her local newspapers – the *Loughborough Monitor* – carried a long interview by Constance Rothery, who made it quite clear that whatever soap Lady Barnett used, she was still a very beautiful lady: 'The eyes are brown with no apparent pupils, the nose most delightfully pert, the mouth and chin definite, and the hair the sort that looks as though it stays where it is put. Lady Barnett was wearing a deceptively simple pale blue suit in an open weave material that had rather clever cuffs, with a faintly-patterned silk blouse.'

After a long assessment of her attributes, Constance Rothery then asked her interviewee if – as a woman who apparently had everything – she had a secret yearning? 'I think I must be a contented sort really because I don't think I have. Everything that has happened to me has happened more by accident than design, you know, being in the right place at the right time. My strongest feeling is that I want to go on working and I don't mind particularly what it is. I like being with people – I like to know what makes them tick, and that is the pleasure of the work I am doing at the moment.'

Her only television work then was a fairly regular invitation to appear with Arthur Negus on BBC Television's antiques programme, 'Going for A Song'. While she enjoyed that very much, mainly because it allowed her to indulge a strong personal interest in antiques, she did seem disenchanted with television in general. She had by then accepted that her screen career was unlikely to be resurrected and she admitted: 'I've been on the box too much over the years and I imagine people were saying that if they saw my face again, they would scream!' She was also conscious that Britain's lifestyle had changed so dramatically since the early 1950s that her kind of elegance and sophistication were no longer much of an attraction. Revelations in the popular Sunday newspapers had by then shown the masses that the rich and the titled suffered from all the weaknesses of the flesh and all the over-indulgences of the common man. Lady Barnett was almost happy to be out of vogue: 'I am simply not one of the four-letter words.' She summed up the general drift of permissiveness and its impact on television since her 'What's My Line?' days with her usual gentility: 'The emphasis then was on the bosom but this seems to have changed. Not long ago I was asked to appear on the programme "Going for a Song" and it was suggested that I bring along just a couple of dresses. I thought this rather odd because I thought I knew all about dressing for television and which dresses photographed well and so on. I soon realised that the outfit was acceptable so long as it showed plenty of knee. The emphasis has descended.'

Lady Barnett seemed to excuse radio from the worst excesses of the sixties and she became almost evangelical about it, telling anyone who would listen – or better still any journalist who would listen and then write about it: 'I like radio better. It's much more my style and you can get more said and more done than on television.' There was, however, an element of rationalization in that comment because while she was working mainly on radio, she never missed an opportunity to appear on television and there is no doubt that if an offer of a new series had come along, she would have taken it. What radio could not give her and television always did was that surge of excitement which she found so heady. The nearest thing to a substitute for that was the minute or so before she spoke to a large audience. In a letter to Molly Cox, she referred to a speech she had made to a huge Women's Institute gathering in the famous Dome at Brighton: 'The hall filled me with terror ... one thousand women stretching apparently to infinity and only one microphone. They were, however, a perfectly blissful audience, warm and quick ... so I enjoyed it.' The feeling was, of course, mutual. Wherever she went – guessing the weight of cakes, drawing raffle tickets, presenting prizes and all the other minutiae of personal appearances – she was always received with genuine affection. What she never lost was the ability to strike up an instant rapport with any group of people. She had an infectious enthusiasm that came across both in the biggest of public halls and in the personal letters to her friend, Molly:

Like you, the pre-Christmas build up caught me on the hop. The final straw, on my only free day, was to dash to London to compère a show for the Not Forgotten Association. One of the artists was Joyce Grenfell and whenever I have anything to do with her I always expect to turn up in one of her sketches. We as always lunched on Christmas Day with great friends of ours who have a mass of children, 5 dogs, 15 macaws, 5 cockatoos, 2 badgers and uncounted assorted white mice, hamsters, and guinea pigs. One of the boys had bought some breathalysers and we tried them out on the men after lunch. Geoffrey, having consumed 1½ glasses of champagne, ditto of claret and one sip of port, turned the thing pale lettuce green, to his horror. The fact that our host turned it jade and the thing nearly blew its top didn't cheer him at all. So I spent the rest of the Christmas parties on nourishing orange juice. I was allowed to drink at our own Christmas Dinner Party here as I only had the stairs to negotiate, and it was thought unlikely that a policeman would be lurking half way up. Still as a result I feel remarkably unhungover, and Alastair is now home for New Year and can take on the driving. I really don't think my red blood corpuscles could take Hogmanay *sans* alcohol.

CHAPTER 13

Despite the outward show of consistent equanimity, much of Lady Barnett's married life had been punctuated by the trauma of watching – with all the punishing awareness of her own medical knowledge – the slow deterioration of her husband's health, and when the illness that had stalked him for so many years finally caught up with Sir Geoffrey in the late 1960s, her worst fears were realized. His shoulders rounded, he found difficulty in walking normally, his speech seemed odd and there was a marked tremor of the hands. She needed no second opinion when his doctor said that these were the symptoms of Parkinson's Disease.

The disease is a chronic condition of the central nervous system which causes nerve cells in certain of the basal ganglia of the brain to degenerate progressively over anything between ten and twenty years. There is no known cure although the use of belladonna drugs can partially alleviate the shaking palsy. Lady Barnett, therefore, had to watch helplessly as her tall, handsome husband was slowly transformed into a stooped, shambling figure, who could no longer walk without scuffing his feet and who often lost his balance and stumbled like a drunk. The disease does not, of course, affect the senses and his intellect was unimpaired. In many ways that, for someone like Sir Geoffrey, is the most cruel aspect of Parkinsonism. To have a razor-sharp mind trapped in a body over which one has decreasing control can only be a constant torment of the worst kind. But whatever they may have said to each other in their intensely-private world, neither Sir Geoffrey nor Lady Barnett ever allowed themselves the luxury of self-pity among even their closest friends. It was another emotional taboo, as they both showed tremendous courage in trying to carry on as normally as possible.

With the aid of his chauffeur-driven Bentley, Sir Geoffrey still went about his business whenever possible and he also insisted on maintaining at least some of their hectic social life. For example, he took Isobel to Italy for her forty-ninth birthday where, as she wrote to Molly Cox: 'We dined to the sound of 23 (?) nightingales. Very romantic.' He sedately followed in the car while she rode with the Quorn Hunt, and they also went, as usual, to Royal Ascot, where one year they were caught in an absolute downpour. Lady Barnett, clearly losing the battle to preserve her hat and dress from the rain, was determined that her shoes at least would not be ruined. She took them off and gaily plodded through the mud bare-footed. With his less extrovert temperament, Sir Geoffrey was not as amused.

Among the commitments that Lady Barnett now decided to give up were her local council work and her role as a magistrate. Lest anyone should connect either withdrawals with her husband's health, she prepared convincing cover stories. Coincidental with boundary changes and massive re-organization, local government had, she maintained, become much too political and she simply stopped enjoying the work because so much was dependent on the party line. As to the magistrates' bench, she was giving up – after twenty years – before she became 'dotty or deaf' as so many of her elderly colleagues had done.

After her death, there was some suggestion that her resignation from the bench was related to her shoplifting problems. There is absolutely no evidence for such a charge and, while it is true to say that because of her enigmatic front nothing can be ruled out, it seems improbable that even she could have kept such a secret for thirteen years. At the time, her overwhelming concern was for her husband, and her self-control was strong enough for her to resist doing anything that might cause him further anguish.

As she tried to spend more and more time at home with Sir Geoffrey, Isobel found a new excitement in manipulating her growing portfolio of investments, and it was a game they could play together. Sir Geoffrey's conservative style and his shrewdness meant that she had a substantial safety-net of building society shares (offering ready availability of cash and marginal tax-relief) and a wide variety of unit trusts, while her own instinct and flair took her into risk companies, from which she got her excitement when the shares increased. She was particularly pleased to have ignored advice and made a handsome profit on her dealings in shares of Tesco, then fast-developing as one of the country's high street supermarket chains. She had also patiently waited for the right time to buy into commercial television, avoiding the initial loss-making years and coming up trumps with the runaway success of Lew Grade's ATV.

Her intuitive dealings were acknowledged by her City associates and when the Family Savings Trust was taken over by the Target Group, she was asked to stay with the new organization as an adviser on consumerism and its likely effect on shares. Basically, they wanted her to keep her finger on the high street pulse – at which she was by now particularly adept – and let them know how the manufacturers and retail chains were performing alongside the demands of Britain's housewives. They must have been particularly comforted by her successes with Tesco, Glaxo and Great Universal Stores.

How shrewd she was in her more personal investments – in antiques and paintings – did not become clear until after her death, when the contents of the White House were auctioned for more than £100,000. But buying good pieces or fine paintings had always excited her and she loved nothing better than trying to outwit the dealers as they struggled to narrow the gap between their prices and what she was prepared to pay. This horse-trading satisfied what she called her Aberdonian parsimony, which was what took her into antiques in the first place: 'I think it's having been born in Aberdeen that it just breaks my heart that the minute a modern piece comes through the door it loses half its value. That doesn't happen with antiques if you buy sensibly!'

While he appreciated her companionship, Sir Geoffrey was anxious not to let his illness interfere too much with Lady Barnett's outside activities, and as she had already retired from the magistrates' bench and the local council, he positively encouraged her to carry on with her radio work and her seemingly never-ending run of personal appearances. That suited her very well, although trying to combine her domestic duties with the other work sometimes proved difficult. Just after getting back from a short holiday, she wrote once more to Molly Cox:

I am labouring mightily in the garden. I arrived home on Saturday at 12 noon, the gardener went on holiday at 12.15 pm – having given me my instructions for the next two weeks. My housekeeper goes away next Thursday and between now and then I have eight recordings to do and three books to read for one of them. One of the books is *Tess of the D'Ubervilles*. Didn't care much for it at school. Haven't changed!

In her letters, Lady Barnett gave no hint of her anxiety about Sir Geoffrey's health and her concern about Alastair and his future showed only in her constant references to his activities:

He joined a male cooking session at the Aylesbury College, but as only two males turned up, Alastair and an elderly widowered vicar, they were asked if they would mind if a few brides joined them as the brides' course was overflowing. Alastair needless to say was delighted (perhaps the vicar was too) and now Geoffrey is worried about breach of promise if Alastair elopes with the best cooking bride of the bunch. He brings home some of his offerings and to see Geoffrey eating a rather lop-sided coconut madelaine minus its cherry (subsequently found on the back seat of his car) is a sight not to be missed. Anyway I don't think he's likely to be revolting!'

Although she never wrote or talked about her own worries, Lady Barnett was always ready to listen to other people's problems and offer them advice or help. In Leicestershire, Mrs Norah Cheatle says: 'She was a wonderful listener and even when she must have been at her most anxious over Geoffrey, she seemed to have the time to care for other people too. I told her all my little worries and she was always very comforting and, of course, always sensible.' When her friend in Scotland, Rosemary Anderson, became ill with a virus infection after a visit to Pakistan, Isobel had her own prescription for the subsequent depression:

I despatched yesterday six quarter bottles of champagne and a large jar of super honey. My prescribing is out of date and non metric but when one is low I'm sure a daily swig of champagne does more for one's morale than Parish's Food [an old-fashioned cure-all].

She was also very sympathetic when Molly Cox's mother went into hospital with cancer early in 1970, and promptly suggested that they met up in the hope that she might ease the worry, at least for a few hours:

Do come on from Kings X to the Bath Club and I will revive you with tea and buns or gin whichever will be most a propos. Don't bother to let me know, I shall be there anyway! I won't gossip on in this letter hoping to exchange it all in person.

The first time she revealed her own worry was in a letter written to Molly Cox on the morning of 18 May, 1970:

Apologies but I have been in despair with Geoffrey. They discovered that his anaemia was due to intestinal bleeding, so took him into the Fielding Johnson Private Hospital and X-rayed him in all directions – nothing. By this time, his haemoglobin was 51° so an exploratory laparotomy had to be done. The surgeon told me to expect a carcinoma and the odds were that it would be inoperable. To everyone's enormous relief they found a little benign adenomatous polyp bleeding away. I was so cock-a-hoop and for two days Geoffrey was in terrific form – then he staged a massive renal failure and for three days we despaired. Seven assorted specialists surrounded him and kept him alive with varying mixtures of drugs by drip, and he gradually came back to the land of the living. He is now very weak but progressing very very slowly.

Even as anxious as she must have been to write so much about her own feelings, she still took the trouble to ask after Molly's two sisters, one who had been ill in America, and the other who had been in hospital in London: 'I'm glad that your father is coping well at home [following the death of Molly's mother]. Really trouble does overwhelm in one ghastly clot, doesn't it!'

Lady Barnett did not realize just how soon she was to be overwhelmed. Later the same day, Sir Geoffrey died.

She was sitting with him in his room at a private nursing home when it happened. For once she did not try to conceal the awful hurt. She told Molly Cox: 'I am bereft to the bottom of my being.' And, for the first time, she was able to cry.

I was so touched by your message and your flowers both for Geoffrey and for me. One other person sent me flowers – Alastair – and both reduced me to very grateful tears. Geoffrey's death came so suddenly and so gently that he knew nothing. It took me a moment to realise. I am so happy on two counts. The first that death was merciful. The alternatives would have been intolerable for him. He was not built to be a dependent invalid. The second was that when I went to see him – there was Geoffrey. Not the anguished tormented invalid, and his beautiful hands were still as he had so wished them to be during the Parkinson years.

For the thirty years they had been married, Lady Barnett had not only loved her husband, she had also admired him tremendously. If it was his tall, dark and handsome appearance that she had fallen for at their first war-time meeting in Nottinghamshire, it was his quiet strength of character that she grew to respect over the years. He had been the sheet-anchor to her impetuous nature and he had gently rubbed smooth most of the sharp edges of her youthful selfishness and thoughtlessness. She was only too aware of how hard he had had to fight to control his own apprehensions, to allow her to pursue her television career at such breakneck speed, and how he had given up some of his own ambitions so as not to interfere with her progress. She was, therefore, very pleased when there was acknowledgement of his considerable public service in Leicestershire:

I have been so moved by the unbelievable kindness. The service was very simple and the Bishop gave the address. His theme 'He was a very parfit gentil knight.' Every Catholic Community in Leicester has sent little notices that Mass is being offered for him and the Rabbi has written to say that tomorrow they will pray for him.

Despite the obvious turmoil of her inner feelings, she still managed to show her usual cool composure to the world. When Sir Geoffrey died, her defence mechanism was triggered into action so quickly that few would have known how badly it had hit her. Her apparent first concern was that the funeral should go off as smoothly as possible. She supervised all the arrangements personally without showing a flicker of emotion. Mrs Sybil Lines, her housekeeper, was amazed by her self-control: 'She was marvellous. We all knew what a terrible blow Sir Geoffrey's death was but she wouldn't even bring in caterers to provide food for all the mourners who came back to the White House from the cemetery.' Instead, Lady Barnett and the regular staff spent hours cutting sandwiches and preparing other food and drinks. That, of course, helped to keep her mind occupied.

Two days after the funeral, she knuckled down to the sad and unenviable job of replying to more than 800 messages of sympathy. Her secretary, Mrs Burton, had to sit and watch: 'She wouldn't let me help very much because, she said, if people had taken the trouble to write to her personally, the very least she could do to show her appreciation was to reply in the same way. It was a mammoth task but she disciplined herself to doing so many letters a day until she got through the long list.'

Among the messages of sympathy was a note from one of her 'Many A Slip' colleagues, Richard Murdoch, and he had enclosed a short tract he had been given by a church friend. She found it so helpful and comforting that she had several copies made to send to other friends.

Death is nothing at all . . . I have only slipped away into the next room . . . I am I and you are you . . . Whatever we were to each other that we are still. Call me by my old familiar name, speak to me in the easy way which you always used. Put no difference into your tone; wear no forced air of solemnity or sorrow. Laugh as we always laughed at the little jokes we enjoyed together. Play, smile, think of me, pray for me. Let my name be ever the household word that it always was. Let it be spoken without an effort, without the ghost of a shadow on it. Life means all that it ever meant. It is the same as it ever was; there is absolutely unbroken continuity. What is this death but a negligible accident? I am but waiting for you, for an interval, somewhere very near, just around the corner. All is well.

Certainly she tried to believe that all was well and she did laugh as she had always laughed. A week after the funeral, she was back on the gruelling public-speaking circuit and at her first function – a Midland women's organization lunch – she spoke with all her usual stylish wit. Few of the guests could have realized she was so-recently widowed. One woman who did congratulate her on having put on a brave face got a phlegmatic reply: 'Well, thank you, but no one has come out to lunch to listen to me being sorry for myself, have they?'

Her grief, however, was not always so easy to contain. Some months after Sir Geoffrey's death, she was in London to record 'Many A Slip' and she met up with an old acquaintance. 'We were sitting talking in her club and somehow the conversation got around to David Nixon and how he had lost his wife in a fatal accident. Suddenly I could see how upset she was and obviously she had been reminded of her own loss. It was the only time I had ever seen her break down and she was so distressed that she asked me to get her chauffeur to bring the car round and she bundled herself into the back seat and was driven off into the night. It was terribly sad.'

Adjusting to life without Sir Geoffrey was far from easy. The problems were not in her public life because with her consistently full diary, she was able to keep herself busy. It was in the deeper recesses of her mind that she suffered, with the realization that for the first time in all her fifty-two years, she was completely on her own. When, on the first anniversary of his death, Molly Cox sympathetically sent a potted plant to the White House, it was clear that the pain was still very raw:

The past two weeks have so mirrored the same weeks last year. The glorious weather, the cherry trees in bloom, the garden he left so reluctantly, his birthday, and now today. A year makes one realise that one is only half a person but the half that is left is kept intact by the loving kindness of friends.

Without her sheet-anchor – as 'only half a person' – she felt that her life lacked focus. If any one of her friends had found themselves in such a predicament, she would have been the first to rush forward with timely and sensible advice. But in this instance, any exhortations of 'doctor, heal thyself' were doomed to failure. She could not help herself. Nor could any of her friends – because she would not let them. Molly Cox, for example, was gently dissuaded from any further expressions of sympathy and understanding: 'In one of our conversations she said something about the old adage: "Do unto others..." not always working. I got the message. While she was always sympathetic to other people, she couldn't bear sympathy herself.'

It was just the same for her other old school friend, Rosemary Anderson: 'You could never be sorry for Isobel because she always made it clear she would rather cope with any problem by herself. Outwardly at least, she was very confident.'

From what was to happen in 1980, it is possible to assume that Lady Barnett never did get over her husband's death, but about a year or so after it happened, Mrs Lines, her housekeeper, felt she had at least turned the corner in overcoming her sadness: 'I know she still missed him very much but she did come round a bit. She bought herself a new car and she began to do a lot of entertaining again. She had lots of actors and actresses among her friends and whenever any of them were appearing at Midland theatres, she would invite them home for lunch or supper.'

Her son, Alastair, was anxious not to leave her on her own too much and he gave up his job to move back to the White House, where a couple of rooms were converted into a comfortable flatlet for him. Having him there seemed to help. It would have been unfair to expect him to fulfil his father's role as her steadying influence – 'I can't put all the weight on him' – but he did give her enough security to immerse herself once more in the routines of broadcasting, public appearances and her charity work. 'That was very important to her,' says Mrs Lines, 'and she used to say to me: "I don't know what I'll do if I do have to give up work." It was what kept her going.'

Over the years, she must have talked to every kind of audience that one could find in Britain – from tiny gatherings in humble parish rooms to huge assemblies in the great public halls; from modest lunches to five-course banquets. But it never seemed to pall on her. She loved her audiences and every one of them, she said, was different. 'The same audience is even different if one pays a return visit. Each audience must be looked upon as a challenge and as a new experience. If you look at it like that, they will never bore you and – hopefully – you will never bore them.' And if she treated them with such professional respect, they repaid her efforts with the continuing warmth and real affection of their response. Her popularity had, somehow, transcended the ephemeral nature of television and it seemed only minimally affected by her long absence – at least on any kind of regular basis – from the small screen. It was that rapport which kept her going.

The press, too, were still very interested in her activities and she was just as keen to give interviews, but it was nearly two years after his death before she would discuss Sir Geoffrey with any journalist. Then, in March 1972, she agreed to talk to the *Sunday Express*. In a long article in the 'Meeting People' series, Sally Brompton offered an updated thumbnail sketch: 'She has reached her mid-fifties with customary grace; still with the elegant good looks and self-assurance which became her trade-mark.' They talked about the days of 'What's My Line?' and how it affected her life, before then turning to Sir Geoffrey's death. Had she got over it? 'It's a case of coming to terms with it and adjusting. You can't go on looking back with sad nostalgia – it's too destructive and too much of a luxury. We were married for nearly 30 years. That is the longest period of my life and therefore the most important. Luckily I was working and able to go on doing so. It was simply a case of building a different kind of life and getting on with it.'

As a reminder that, at fifty-three, she was still a young widow, she was asked if she might marry again. Her reply was firm: 'Definitely not – 30 years is too long. Besides – I'm a very difficult person to marry. It's not very easy to be married to someone who is on radio or television. My husband used to cope with it with great good humour but most men would hate it. I don't think anyone would want to marry me, anyway.'

Lady Barnett was being modest. She was still very attractive and certainly many of her acquaintances saw her as being eminently eligible. According to Mrs Cheatle, several hostesses contemplated lining up 'suitable' partners for her when they invited her to dinner. 'She absolutely hated that. Whenever she heard that someone had a nice man in mind for her to partner, she would refuse the invitation. She would snort: "Bloody cheek – if I want a man, I'll find my own, thank you!" Of course, she never did. She never contemplated re-marrying. No one would ever have measured up to her estimation of Geoffrey.'

Then, in 1973, there came a major boost for her morale: 'What's My Line?' was to be brought back and the BBC wanted her once more to join the panel.

CHAPTER 14

Lady Barnett was just as hesitant about accepting this invitation as she had been over the original one twenty years earlier. The reasons, of course, were quite different. In 1953, she had worried about how she, an unknown housewife, would fit in with the show's famous personalities. In 1973, now a household name herself, she was dubious about trying to put the clock back: 'You should never go back,' she said. 'Let the past be.' But, of course, she could not resist the opportunity to experience once again the excitement of the television studio, and she agreed to join Anna Quayle, Bill Franklin and Kenneth Williams as the new panel for a limited five-week run on BBC 2. She was, however, cautious about the likely outcome: 'The days of instant success are over,' she told the *Daily Telegraph*. 'I don't think reputations will be made overnight as they were in the 1950s. I don't think it would ever happen again so quickly.' Was she worried now about becoming a national institution if the show was again successful? 'We produce very few. I'd never become *that*! It's just that the comeback is a challenge. It's fun and I always enjoyed the game.'

She was right. There was no instant success for the re-vamped show, but most people were surprised by the size of the audience. It had, said the BBC, all started as a kind of a giggle, but James Thomas was able to write in the *Daily Express* after four of the planned five weeks: 'Giggle or not, the BBC found themselves with nearly seven million viewers for a programme which first hit the small screen nearly 23 years ago. Now it looks as though they will have to resurrect the old war-horse for a longer series.'

In the end it ran for twenty weeks and Lady Barnett enjoyed herself immensely. 'It's a strange combination of feeling partly that one has never been away at all, and yet on the other hand, it is interestingly different just because you are working with new people.' She was also delighted with the resumption of her fan mail, though not in quite the same torrents as before, and she was particularly pleased that much of it came from viewers too young to remember the original series. What she enjoyed most, of course, was the old buzz as the adrenalin flowed: 'There is always – and really I think there ought to be – a tension on the show. If there is none, it will be so relaxed it will be a bad show.'

Her need for excitement – 'I simply pant for excitement,' she wrote as an undergraduate back in the 1930s – never changed and in her broadcasting work she was always keen to do live programmes: 'They are really much more fun. There is much more immediacy when you know you're actually on the air and not just making a recording.' That was why she enjoyed radio's 'Any Questions?' so much: 'You have got to watch your words, of course, otherwise you can be sued for libel and get yourself into very considerable trouble. But that just adds to the tension of the programme.'

As the style of 'Any Questions?' changed – panellists were no longer used on a regular basis – and programmes like 'Twenty Questions' and 'Petticoat Line' disappeared, Lady Barnett's broadcasting opportunities dwindled, but she still found herself driving between speaking engagements every bit as regularly as she had done at the height of her success in the late 1950s. She also acted as question-master at local quizzes around Leicestershire and took time off to collaborate with city journalist, Jack Meadows, in writing *Lady Barnett's Quizbook*, a comprehensive little paperback which told you all you needed to know if you wanted to bring the excitement of 'What's My Line?' or something similar to your own church hall!

Finding that she had more spare time on her hands than before, she developed her interest in bridge – already one of her long-term pleasures – into a consuming passion and played at every opportunity, finding a genteel competitiveness that seemed to keep her spirit alive. Mrs Cheatle, a regular partner, said she was great fun to play with: 'She enjoyed herself so much it was wonderful to watch. She nearly always laughed and giggled through the rubbers and you might have thought she was not taking it seriously . . . until the points were added up!'

It is the Lady Barnett laugh – long and throaty with her head thrown back – that people remember most. In even the most crowded parties, you could always tell where she was by the chain reaction to her infectious chuckles and guffaws. At dinner parties, her end of the table was where the most animated conversations took place, though hers was seldom the dominant voice. 'She was simply a brilliant dinner guest to have,' says Mrs Cheatle, 'because she was such a good listener. She had the widest possible array of conversation pieces herself, but she was always very gracious and listened so intently to what other people had to say that she acted as a catalyst and brought the best out in everyone.'

She was a good listener mainly because she was totally fascinated by people. Her secretary, Mrs Burton, says she always wanted to know how they ticked: 'No matter who they were, she wanted to know more about them. I'm sure if she'd seen a tramp walking along a country lane, she would have stopped to talk to him and find out what he was doing, where he was going, what he was thinking. She always wanted to know what made people the way they were.'

The psychologists, of course, will say that what she was really seeking was self-knowledge. If she found it, she certainly did not reveal it to anyone else. No one, for example, can say why such a gregarious, extrovert woman should want to keep her personal feelings so intensely private, far beyond the usual well-bred British reluctance to talk about oneself; nor just how tough she really was behind her mask of feminine gentility. It is not even possible to say whether or not she suffered from the loneliness that followed Sir Geoffrey's death. Her letters to Molly Cox do not offer any evidence on that score, and while some of her friends think it hit her badly, others, like Mrs Cheatle, say she coped very comfortably: 'Isobel said she adored having the house to herself. Don't forget she was so self-sufficient. She loved reading and whenever you telephoned she said she'd had her nose in one gripping book or another. Either that or she would be wrapped up in a piece of music from one of her vast collection of records.'

For every friend who saw her as an independent, self-contained woman able to cope comfortably on her own, there was someone else with different perceptions. One, for example, said: 'I think she was a very lonely person. You see, she cared so much about other people's loneliness and you just felt her concern arose from personal experience. I remember telling her about a well-known actor and his wife, who lived not far from me. He was away a lot and I often wanted to ring the wife and invite her round for coffee and a chat. I never did, of course, because I was scared of appearing pushy. Isobel seemed quite sad and assured me that if only I'd had the courage, I would have been welcomed with open arms. She wouldn't have said that unless she was pretty sure she was right.'

Molly Cox feels that she missed the kind of companionship that goes with a big extended family: 'She never appeared envious or jealous of my three sons. On the contrary, she was always interested in what they were doing and how they were growing up. But I got the impression that she missed the closeness of the large family circle of her childhood.'

Another friend, the Honourable Mrs Elizabeth Fraser – they met when Lady Barnett was on a lecture trip on the Queen Elizabeth II – also felt that she would have liked a bigger family: 'One weekend I was staying at the White House and I had just changed for dinner, Isobel saw me at the top of the staircase and immediately stopped me walking down the stairs. "Do wait a moment until I get down," she said, "I must have a look at you. The staircase is so splendid and I've never had a daughter to come down it as a bride." It was quite a poignant moment and such a shame. I'm sure she longed for a daughter to share all the pretty things she loved so much.'

For Mrs Lines, the housekeeper, it was the very size of the White House that emphasized Lady Barnett's loneliness: 'She must have felt it at night whenever Alastair was away and the other daily staff and I had gone home . . . she was alone in that big house. All her hectic social activities and all her friends wouldn't help then, would they?'

One must set against that Lady Barnett's own words. Not only did she tell Mrs Cheatle that she liked having the house to herself; she was also quoted on several occasions as saying that one of her favourite times was in the wee small hours – surely the worst time of all for the really lonely? – when she could finally escape from the telephone and go to bed to curl up with all the newspapers: 'It's the only way I can catch up with what's going on in the world!' There is also the fact that she cheerfully – or, at least, apparently so – dissuaded Alastair from staying at home too much. He had become an enthusiastic traveller since giving up his job and she encouraged him to go on trips whenever possible.

Whatever it may have been like at night, the White House was never coloured by loneliness or unhappiness during the day time. It was, says secretary Jeanne Burton, a wonderful place to work. Life seemed to centre around the kitchen, and the day for Lady Barnett and all the staff, plus any odd workmen who happened to be around, was punctuated by copious cups of coffee: 'We all sat at the kitchen table and Lady B – that's what we all called her – would regale us with stories of her travels and her experiences at some of the functions she attended.' There was an office, but she could only be persuaded to go in there to sort out her lecture notes at the very last minute. 'She wasn't always well organised,' says Mrs Burton, 'and she would never remember, for example, where she had left her cigarette seconds after taking it from her lips. There were often half-smoked cigarettes everywhere. It might have looked chaotic but it was always great fun. She was a super person.'

For daily help, Angela Stoneman, she seemed more like an aunt than an employer: 'She was lovely to work for, really easy-going. You could just go in and get on with things in your own way at your own pace. When she sat down with you at coffee she would just talk about her life and I always felt I could confide in her. She would talk to me and advise me and I'd always go home feeling much better.'

By now, Lady Barnett's health was causing her major problems. For years, like so many doctors, she had ignored all the warning signs that she ought to be slowing down a bit and, of course, she resisted suggestions from friends like Molly Cox that she should take it easy: 'Doctors never look after themselves properly and she would never rest, however poorly she felt. She was the exact opposite of a hypochondriac and would never go near a doctor's surgery if she could help it.'

Her first worry was about a thyroid condition which played havoc with her metabolism and caused a fairly dramatic loss of weight. Then she developed an arthritic knee and for several years was in constant pain. In both instances, her medical knowledge worked against her. She was afraid to have anything done about her thyroid because she knew that there was a strong possibility that the goitre which caused so much discomfort – making it difficult for her to swallow or breathe, and probably deepening her voice even more – could be cancerous. Having gone through the nightmare of thinking that Sir Geoffrey might have had a malignant growth, she could not face the prospect of being told that she herself might have cancer. Even so, there was not the slightest let-up in her furious smoking habits.

In the end, because the pain in her throat began to interfere with her lectures and after-dinner speeches, she finally submitted to medical attention. After a quick diagnosis, she slipped into hospital, had a *benign* goitre removed and was discharged again with few of her friends even aware of where she had been.

It was not so easy with the arthritis. Unlike the goitre, everyone could see exactly what was wrong with her knee and there is no doubt that an operation could have helped. Again, however, she knew from some of her medical friends that there was still an element of experimentation in the replacement of arthritic joints, and she refused point-blank to undergo another operation until, she said, they had got it absolutely right. She would rather put up with the pain. 'She was in agony a lot of the time,' says Mrs Burton, 'and you could see her leg swell enormously, but she wouldn't have anything done about it. The trouble was that with her background, she thought she knew what was best for her and, as in everything else, she had the final say in the matter.'

It was the way she coped with the pain that impressed Norah Cheatle: 'Sometimes the leg was so bad you could actually see it bow out as she put her weight on it. Yet she never complained and seemed to accept the pain as just one of the problems of growing old.' Nor would she allow the pain to interfere with her work, which now consisted almost entirely of speaking engagements. Unless they noticed the 'Disabled' badge that suddenly appeared on her car windscreen, few in the audiences that she spoke to would have realized her difficulties. She still stood up while she talked – and that could mean being on her feet for anything up to ninety minutes – and she spoke with the same vigour and enthusiasm.

Certainly she was no less popular as a guest-speaker, and a glance through her diary for 1978 – two years before she died and at the height of her health problems – shows that she was as busy as ever with engagements throughout the year all over Britain. In one week, for example, she went to speak in Penrith, Cardiff and Cornwall and in another she was in Herne Bay, Edinburgh, Cornwall and Burton-on-Trent. She was sixty and her travelling that year took her nearly 40,000 miles, most of which she drove herself.

During this period Lady Barnett was developing a new friendship which seemed to offer more scope in her continuing quest for self-knowledge. It was an improbable relationship that began when she met the newly-appointed Provost of Leicester, the Very Reverend Alan Warren, at various public functions around the city. It was improbable because she was an agnostic – despite her Presbyterian upbringing and Quaker education – and he was one of the pillars of the Church of England: 'It was quite remarkable really. She was highly critical of the church as an institution, while I was one of the defenders of the Faith . . . an Establishment man.'

Despite their different stances, they were soon having long, serious conversations: 'She came into my study one day, sat down and without any preamble said: "Provost, I want to talk to you about this problem of suffering." I was quite taken aback because I thought she was going to offer to open a garden fête for me or something like that. Really there are very few people in any walk of life who could come in and, without any messing about, launch into such a discussion. What she wanted to know was if suffering could ever be redemptive – that's putting it in theological terms – and we then talked quite a bit about suffering. She had known suffering in her own life. She said, for example, how deeply she felt her husband's death. It had been a very, very great shock for her but she felt she had come through it and had learned to cope.'

Life-after-death was another topic Lady Barnett raised with the Provost and again, Sir Geoffrey was in her thoughts: 'She had a naïve vision of Heaven and still thought of it as the place where she could have her husband with her. I tried to explain that Heaven was not just an extension of this life. You don't just go up to Heaven where you see a transmogrified granny and grandad in front of a transmogrified television set watching the news. As Jesus says, there's no marriage there. It isn't necessary . . . it's a totally new dimension, a totally new relationship.'

It is quite likely that many of her friends will be surprised to learn of these conversations because she gave so little away in talking to them: 'She was conscious that in her relationships with other people she was kind of superficial,' says Mr Warren, 'and she wanted more than that. There was in her an insecurity, as if she was searching for something deeper but she didn't quite know what she was looking for.'

On one occasion, she asked him if he would say a prayer for her. 'It was a very unusual thing for her to do but we just sat there together very quietly and prayed together. Isobel wasn't a person of faith in the orthodox sense, but as the New Testament says, faith is the substance of something hoped for. Real faith is not in *knowing* the answers, it's in reaching out. She had this kind of faith. She said she was not afraid of death and she often talked to me about the idea of life as a sort of preparation. She wanted to know if this life was really, a training ground for the next – a prelude, perhaps, to something greater in the future.'

Lady Barnett's interest in a hereafter was clearly bound up

with how much she missed the support of her husband. In the tract she had received from Richard Murdoch, it was its implication for her that Sir Geoffrey was 'somewhere very near, just around the corner' that had given so much comfort. In her conversations with the Provost, she often said she felt Sir Geoffrey was helping her to overcome her difficulties and that she particularly felt his presence in the White House.

This deeper side to her nature was very well screened and her public attitude towards the church bordered on cynicism. She was particularly critical of the big civic occasions when the church seemed, in her words, to welcome 'all those pompous old so and sos' just to keep the other half of the establishment happy. Mr Warren's response to such comments were to remind her that Jesus found time for Nickodemus as well as for the fishermen: 'I think sometimes the very things she criticized the most were those in which she really wanted to be involved.'

Her main criticism of the church as a whole was one based on her own needs: 'She thought the church wasn't exciting enough. She longed for excitement in many things but I think she found it hard to control and accept when she got there. There is in all this, of course, something of an enigma about ... maybe there is something of an enigma that you just have to leave there.'

When the shop-lifting charges were first made, one would have expected her to turn to Mr Warren if to no one else: 'She did know me well enough and I think she did trust me enough to know that I would never break a confidence, but around the time of the trial all she said was, "You don't think I would risk my reputation stealing all these trivial little things?" and I accepted that.' Now, of course, he can see why she was so upset by the jury's decision: 'Deep down in the heart of her she was still really a child. She had a need to be sheltered and supported and loved by everyone.'

There has been much speculation about how long Lady Barnett had been shoplifting before the local shop-keeper reported her to the police in 1980 – and even more, of course, about why she should do it. With claims ranging from two to fifteen years – discounting those who still believe it never happened – it is difficult, against the background of her active routine, to pinpoint when it started. Even today, the shopkeepers around Leicestershire are reluctant to say how long their protective conspiracy of silence lasted other than 'for a few years'. The rumours, however, began in 1978 and they were compounded by the hints from more malicious gossips that the lady from the White House also had a drink problem. The irony is that, because of her health problems, there appeared to be more substance in this latter story than in the shoplifting allegations. She sometimes did stagger as she got out of her car and put her weight on her arthritic knee, and she was occasionally dazed by the powerful painkillers she took.

Everyone close to her completely discounts any idea that she might have been an alcoholic. Norah Cheatle probably spent more time with her than anyone else in the last few years and would have spotted any drink problem immediately: 'We all enjoyed drinking socially and Isobel was no different from the rest of us. She usually drank white wine and she certainly never drank too much. I can tell you how unimportant it was to her from a holiday we spent at my villa in Spain with two other friends. It was one of our regular bridge foursomes and one of the other women kept on winning. On the plane back, Isobel spent most of the flight trying to inveigle this woman to buy the drinks, not because she wanted one but because she wanted her money back in one form or another! She wouldn't have a drink from anyone else as a matter of principle. When she finally managed to squeeze an offer out of our friend, the captain ruined it all by insisting that the drinks were on him! Isobel was quite cross but then she had the good grace to send him a thank you note – written on the sick-bag and signed "Four grateful old ladies". She wouldn't have had time for all that if she'd needed a drink.'

Another friend is equally certain, because of a promise Isobel made to Sir Geoffrey: 'They were joking around one evening and when he seemed uncertain about her state, she quickly reassured him by showing that she was only pretending to be tipsy, and then she added the simple promise that she would never ever open a bottle on her own. Isobel always kept her promises and she would never have let Geoffrey down.'

If there was no substance in the drink story, sadly there was truth in the rumours about shoplifting.

An old school friend who did not live in Leicestershire, was totally unaware of the gossip, but in retrospect realizes that there were clues two or three years before Lady Barnett's death: 'Queer things begin to make sense now. When I was staying with Isobel about three years before she died, we were out to dinner when the host started asking me about her schooldays, with questions about whether or not she had ever got into any kind of trouble. I thought it was all just dinner-table small-talk until Isobel said quite coldly: "You've got the wrong friend there." I didn't make anything of it at the time, but now I realise that it was her Celtic sixth-sense at work. She thought that I had that sixth-sense too, and would therefore be aware of her problems. In her mind, the man was pumping me for information and her interruption was her way of thanking me for not falling for it."

Mrs Cox's relationship with Lady Barnett was, as her letters show, very special. After school in York, they never lived in the same area as each other, but remained close friends through the long-running correspondence: 'Isobel was always incredibly sensitive to my moods and emotions and she often anticipated them. Our letters were forever crossing. Even after gaps of months, I would decide to write and the very next day there would be an envelope on the mat in her neat handwriting. It was uncanny.' Mrs Cox also feels that Lady Barnett knew that someone would want to write her biography one day and that the letters would be relevant. About fifteen years ago, she returned the early letters she had received, but Lady Barnett gave them back, saying: 'They're yours, not mine.' Mrs Cox got the impression she meant: 'To do with as you think best.'

Mrs Cox also has what she calls a 'snapshot' recollection of what she feels may have been one of Lady Barnett's shoplifting escapades: 'I was staying with her at the White House and we were sitting talking when she suddenly jumped up, saying she needed some things and would I care for a drive. I agreed and she ushered me into the car so quickly that I forgot to pick up my handbag. We drove away from Cossington and, as it happened, we went past the house where she had lived with her in-laws. Geoffrey was obviously in her mind and she spoke about him as if he were still there [other friends say she often talked about him in the present tense] although it was clear she was only reminiscing. She spoke of her sadness when her mother-in-law had suggested exchanging that dark Victorian house for the smaller sunnier one she and Geoffrey had chosen. However she did say that the White House compensated later for that early disappointment.

'We finally stopped in a nearby village where she took me into a little, old-fashioned shop with lots of nooks and crannies. The atmosphere struck me as odd. The assistants just stood and watched. They didn't come forward, as I would have expected. I decided I'd like to look for a present for her and went off to browse among the shelves. I realized then I didn't have my handbag and therefore hadn't got any money with me. I turned to look for Isobel and came up behind her in another alcove. She had an unusual bottle of wine in her hand, but as soon as she saw me she put it back on the shelf and said something about it being too expensive. I had a strange feeling at the time that she was behaving oddly, but quickly dismissed it and didn't think of it again until after her death. I wonder now if she would have taken that bottle had I not come up behind her?'

At the time, of course, Mrs Cox – like her other friends – had not the slightest notion that Lady Barnett was under any undue stress. It is true that her health problems, particularly the pain, had begun to leave their marks and she was looking much older, but it happened fairly gradually and Mrs Cox, who saw her about once a year, assumed the change in her was due to her arthritic knee. 'I was a year older than Isobel but I thought I looked much more, so it came as a shock when a broadcasting colleague of hers once asked me if I'd really been at school with Isobel because I looked ten years younger. That was only a few months after Geoffrey's death, which seemed to explain the change in her.'

Rosemary Anderson came from Glasgow to visit her friend in 1979, not having seen her for a couple of years, and was quite shocked: 'She agreed to meet me off the coach but when we arrived at the bus station there was no sign of her. It was very unusual for her to be late for anything and I stood around wondering if I was in the right place or had the wrong date or something. Then I heard her voice calling me and I hardly recognised her. Her hair had turned white and she was terribly lame. It was very sad.'

If the flesh had weakened, the spirit certainly had not. Lady Barnett was still a willing slave of her diary, and no organization to whom she spoke could have felt short-changed. When she was dressed for the occasion, she was still an attractive woman, and when the expectant hush descended on her audience she delivered her talk with all the style and wit for which they had paid.

She was also still one of the press's favourite ladies although it was no longer her physical attributes that caught their attention. In a *My Weekly* of March 1979, Syd Gillingham wrote: 'The voice is unmistakeable. The rich, elegant tones seem to caress the words rather than merely speak them.' And then he used a quote that was equally unmistakeable, with all the hallmarks of her delightful, self-denigrating humour: 'Now I'm getting old and grey and not much on the telly, I can go about with not too many people knowing who I am – until I open my mouth!'

One of the last national articles to be written about her before her death pleased Lady Barnett even more than most, appearing as it did in the *British Medical Journal*, where, under other circumstances, she might have published her learned papers. Under the 'In and Out of Medicine' column, the journal traced her career from medical school to broadcasting: 'Practically everything she does is connected with meeting people and she has almost managed to overcome (or at least mask) the residual shyness that afflicts so many doctors ... she says that everything she has done has been accidental and she has never had an original thought in her life.' As always, her modesty and honesty came across and she readily confessed to a lack of purpose in her life: 'She regrets that she has no particular day-to-day crusade at the moment and wonders what she should do next.' The journal offered its own remedy: 'Why doesn't someone suggest that she combines her knowledge of medicine and the media by teaching medical students and doctors how to talk to and listen to their patients? She is charming and alert and eminently suitable for such a task.'

If only ... if only someone had taken up that suggestion, things might have been so different. As it was, she carried on apparently aimlessly according to her friend Elizabeth Fraser: 'There was an enormous gap in her life from the time Geoffrey died right up until her own death. She tried to hide it. She never talked about herself. It was nearly always about her television success and all the famous people she had met. But you could tell that you were only being allowed to see the façade and that there was a private side which you were never allowed to see.'

The one thing that did come along and capture her interest was the Independent Broadcasting Authority's opening of bids for a new commercial radio station in Leicester. It was right up her street and she rose willingly to the challenge. She got together with a group of local businessmen, politicians and other broadcasters, and under her able chairmanship, they put together an attractive prospectus for a homespun local community service. With all her usual energy and enthusiasm, she canvassed the IBA in her group's interests, and in May 1980 she heard that they had won the franchise and her company would be able to start broadcasting as Centre Radio sometime early in 1981.

If only ... if only the project had come up a year earlier, again things could have been so different. It was an exciting development which could well have given her a new sense of purpose. At the very least the hard work and commitment needed would have reduced the gap in her life, possibly to manageable proportions. But by the time the good news arrived in Leicester, it was apparently too late for Lady Barnett. Try as she might to shrink from the reality – and she did by carrying on as if nothing had happened – other events had begun to catch up with her. Although it was still a well kept secret, she had already been reported to the police for shoplifting. A month later it became public when she was formally charged. Two months after that came the magistrates' hearing and the astonishing decision to go for trial by jury. Another two months and she was in the dock, to be found guilty of stealing a carton of cream and a tin of fish. Four days later, alone in the big empty White House, late at night – the very circumstances in which, her housekeeper said, she must have felt the worse effects of loneliness – she killed herself.

It was a grim timetable and even today, after the embers of her life have been raked over by the gossips, the friends and the experts, no one can say when the countdown really began – or why.

INDEX